Use this pattern...

mmmmmmm
mmmmmmmmmmm
mmmmmmmmmmm

...for these letters.

n m r h k b p

Related letters:

i j s f x z

A MANUAL FOR

fluent hand-writing

NAN JAY BARCHOWSKY

Published by

Aberdeen Maryland USA

BFH, A Manual for Fluent Handwriting

by Nan Jay Barchowsky

Copyright © 1997 by Nan Jay Barchowsky. All rights reserved. No part of this book may be reproduced or transmitted in any form, or by any means, without the express written permission of the author.

Neither the author, nor the publisher will be held responsible for any injury, loss or other damage incurred by any reader, user, student, or group of students as a result of the use of this book.

Library of Congress Catalog Card Number: 97-091564

ISBN 0-9656745-7-6

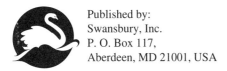

Published by:
Swansbury, Inc.
P. O. Box 117,
Aberdeen, MD 21001, USA

Design by Paul and Nan Jay Barchowsky
First Printing
Printed in the United States of America

ACKNOWLEDGMENT

In 1975, Sara Weymouth Brumfield, the head and a founder of Harford Day School, an independent elementary school, asked me to do something about the alphabets that were displayed in the classrooms. The school needed new exemplars. Those on the market had too many curlicues for her taste. A discussion of handwriting ensued. One thing led to another, and I became the handwriting advisor and teacher for the school. My devotion to the improvement of handwriting instruction has grown steadily ever since.

To Sara Brumfield, Harford Day School, its teachers and students, I owe the opportunity to explore an approach to better handwriting instruction. The exploration has been rewarding. Former students now enjoy their handwriting for all its various uses, including the ability to take quick, effective notes.

It is often noted that through teaching, one learns. I learned that most students do not want to emulate a model hand. They want their individuality to show in their handwriting. At the same time, they need to develop a hand that is legible and fast.

Model characters are necessary tools. However, most, if not all, handwriting manuals provide boring copybooks with page after page for students to trace and copy. Such books may have been a good idea in the nineteenth century, when it was trace and copy, or be whacked on the wrist with a ruler. Whacking is no longer an option for teachers. Today's teachers are overburdened with required curricula, and are ill prepared to teach handwriting with the necessary understanding of the physiological attributes of the skill. Attention to physiology can solve many problems, including aching hands, and even reversals. "Form follows function" is too often disregarded.

My classroom observations taught me the relationship of good posture, pen hold, and paper position, as well as the way the body is positioned, to the relaxed, easy movement that makes handwriting fluent. Dr. Rosemary Sassoon, a handwriting specialist in Great Britain, reinforced my awareness of the physical capabilities and needs of students.

I am deeply and sincerely grateful to Dr. Sassoon, and to Sheila Waters, Tom Gourdie, Dr. Lawrence Wheeler, Katherine Dallam, and Sally V. McGrath for their helpful criticism and support.

To my husband, Paul, I owe an immeasurable debt for his support and advice.

TABLE OF CONTENTS

INTRODUCTION

I   **POSTURE, PEN OR PENCIL HOLD, AND PAPER POSITION** 1
     Several illustrations accompany the instructions.

II   **EXERCISE PATTERNS, RELATED LETTERS & PRACTICE WORDS** 7
     A variety of patterns pertain to and train movement for the formation of characters.

III   **REFERENCE FOR LOWERCASE ALPHABET** 11

IV   **REFERENCE FOR CAPITAL ALPHABET** 25

V   **REFERENCE FOR NUMERALS** 37

VI   **JOINING LETTERS** 41
     Ligatures are explained and presented in the order in which they should be introduced, starting with the ones that assist legibility and those that are the easiest and most natural, and moving to those that may or may not be made according to the preferences of individuals. Some ligatures are detrimental to legibility and/or speed. These are described.

VII   **HINTS AND COMPARISONS WITH OTHER WRITING SYSTEMS** 51
     Teachers and older students may have learned to write by other methods. Teachers who understand the differences between the method or methods they learned can best assist their students to improve their handwriting, or if necessary, to adjust their handwriting to the methods in this manual. Suggestions for the remediation of some common handwriting problems are also included.

VIII   **USING BARCHOWSKY™ FLUENT HAND™ TYPE** 63
     Unjoined letters in Barchowsky™ Fluent Hand™ are typed on a keyboard just as one would type with any other font. In order to produce exemplars with joined letters, one must use the alternate keystrokes in Barchowsky™ Fluent Hand™. There is an explanatory text.

IX   **PRACTICE WORDS AND SENTENCES** 73
     This section has suggestions for sequences of letters to practice.

APPENDIX
     Glossary 81
     Supplements and the CD-ROM 83

INTRODUCTION

BFH Throughout this manual BFH refers to Barchowsky Fluent Hand, the method, and to the font, Barchowsky™ Fluent Hand™. BFH, the method, is dedicated to maximum legibility with maximum speed. With the program in this manual, students develop handwriting that will serve them for the rest of their lives.

Children should establish habits of the simplest, possible movements to form characters when they first start to scribble. Fluent, adult handwriting relies upon early training of small muscles to move rhythmically and consistently.

Children are eager to learn. It is necessary to communicate basic needs in order to survive. Just as soon as babies realize they can elicit responses, they proclaim each new communication skill with a joy and delight that is seldom matched beyond the tenderest years. They observe everything with fresh, new light, question everything. They gurgle and chatter tirelessly, and try out each sound they hear until eventually they master understandable language.

Next come marks. Anything that makes its mark on any surface is magic to be explored. When marks evolve into the letters of a child's name, he or she is exhilerated by the accomplishment. Young children, while playing, can learn with little effort the essential movements that create the letters of names and other words. All the while they are reinforcing directional and spacial concepts and color recognition.

The BFH program introduces joined (cursive) writing by age six or seven. Children then have the tools to freely express all their wondrous imaginings with pencil and paper. They can be rightfully proud of their ability to state their thoughts easily, and with visual clarity. Youngsters are thereby inspired to develop all academic skills, from creative writing to science and math.

It is the responsibility of all instruction to nurture an eagerness to learn, to help children experience the excitement and rewards of discovery, thought, and self-expression throughout their lives. To instruct any subject, one must understand that subject. In the case of handwriting, consider your own. When and how do *you* handwrite? How do your thoughts about handwriting compare with those of your colleagues? A keyboard may satisfy all of your needs except for those occasions when handwriting is the only appropriate way to go. Or you may be one who thinks best with pen in hand. Perhaps you enjoy writing letters by hand for the intimacy and expressiveness when you communicate with family and friends. You may be a poet, and want the sensual immediacy of handwriting. Almost everyone needs note-taking skills. Any of these needs or preferences will also be those of students, and the handwriting instruction they receive should not preclude any of them.

The first part of the introduction is in the author's personal hand. Now you are reading Barchowsky™ Fluent Hand™, the font with which teachers or parents can quickly produce exemplary lesson plans that complement the studies or interests of students.

Barchowsky™ Fluent Hand™ is the model used in this manual. A model is necessary for beginners. However, a student should be encouraged to move away from emulating a model as soon as possible, and to begin the development of an individual style of writing, limited only by the stroke directions and sequences that foster clear and rapid writing—not necessarily "beautiful" writing. Handwriting that is legible and looks neat (perhaps some would think "beautiful") may have been painstakingly drawn. Habits of movement formed with unduly slow writing will prove a hindrance to fluency in later years. It is easy, enjoyable handwriting for which we ultimately strive.

Handwriting must be legible or it is worthless. It must be reasonably fast, or the writer will condemn it as near worthless.

BFH, a Manual for Fluent Handwriting offers detailed information on posture, paper position, and exercise patterns to facilitate rhythmic movement and the formation of characters. Lesson plans are included. However, teachers are encouraged to alter the plans, adapting them to the needs of a class or individual. Handwriting instruction should relate to curricula. Once children learn to form letters and numerals, separate classes can be counterproductive, sending a message that good handwriting is required only in that class, not in all writing. Legible handwriting at a reasonable speed should be required in all classes.

At all stages students learn discipline—that word may elicit visions of a nineteenth century schoolmaster with his charges. It need not. When seasoned with thought and consideration for the students, discipline can be an agreeable matter. Although often neglected, discipline is essential for success in the world, and the twenty-first century will be no exception.

Finally, in an ideal world, teachers should have to read only legible assignments. But some papers will be hard to decipher—the signal that the writer needs help. This manual offers solutions to illegibility.

Nan Jay Barchowsky

SECTION I

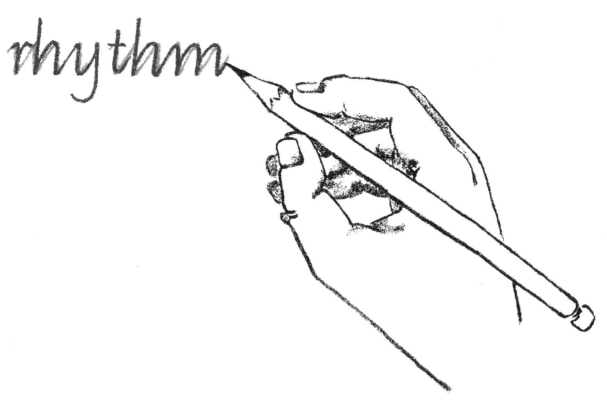

POSTURE, PEN OR PENCIL HOLD AND PAPER POSITION

Write effortlessly!

Pull the chair close to the desk and directly in front of it. Clear the desk top. Sit with the torso straight, but not rigid, and leaning slightly forward. A hand should just fit between the back of the chair and the back of the writer.

Legs and feet should be in a position that will not throw the body to one side; the feet may be crossed but not the legs. Part of both forearms should rest on the desk, but not the elbows. When an elbow rests on the desk, it tends to lock the upper body into one position, which is off center, and movement is restricted.

To better understand the relationship of pencil hold to letter formation, it is worth noting that some handwriting instruction, such as the Palmer method, teaches students to allow only the tips of the third, ring and little fingers and the forearm near the elbow to touch the desk. This posture results in whole arm movement, and the joining of every letter becomes reasonable. However, it is rare to see anyone writing with this posture. This method of writing was introduced in the nineteenth century. Since that time both writing tools and demands on our time have changed dramatically.

Try holding your arm and hand in the position just described, as you write with a ballpoint pen. Write a few long words, such as **alphabetically**, **extemporaneously**, **candlesnuffers**, **zingerbaceous**. Usually the heel of the hand wants to rest on the desk or paper. Unless one lifts the pen or pencil after writing a few letters, one tends to drag the heel of the hand on the paper. Letters become distorted, tension increases, and fluency goes out the window.

A writing instrument should be held loosely. The illustration on the previous page shows a recommended placement of the fingers on a pencil. This manual is not adamant about a precise pen or pencil hold, other than that it must be relaxed. The writing instrument is controlled by the forefinger, held between it and the thumb, and supported by the third finger. The other two fingers are underneath. The writing instrument should rest in the cradle formed by the meeting of the thumb and forefinger. The non-writing end of the pen or pencil should point over the right shoulder for right-handers. For maximum control, the tip of the forefinger should be about one inch (two and one half centimeters) from the point of the pen or pencil (on a sharpened pencil, the forefinger is on the paint, just above the shaved part).

Left-handed writers should follow the same instructions as those given to right-handers, with a few exceptions. In order to maintain a comfortable position without a hooked wrist, the non-writing end of the pen or pencil will point further out from the body. The forefinger should be moved up on the shaft of the writing tool by about one fourth of an inch (seven millimeters) for good control.

Illustrations for both right and left-handers will be found in the CD-ROM supplementary material for the user of this manual to copy. They are intended as exemplars for students, to be used at the same size or blown-up to poster size. When displayed, the illustrations should be posted at an angle to demonstrate proper position of the paper. See pages four, five and six.

Marks should be made principally by the pressure of the forefinger against the writing instrument. The marks are modified into various letterforms by the movement of the whole hand. Excess pressure on the pen or pencil invariably results in tense writing that will not flow rapidly, clearly, or comfortably.

Many people hold writing instruments in a death grip with various odd placements of fingers on their writing tools. Have they adjusted, with no guidance, to ballpoints that make a mark only when held upright? Dr. Rosemary Sassoon, who works extensively with handwriting problems, suggests a means to a more relaxed hold. It works especially well for long fingers and for some left-handers. Please note the illustration on page five. The writing instrument is still controlled by the thumb and forefinger, with the remaining fingers in much the same position as previously described, but it is placed between the forefinger and third finger. Any pen resting between these two fingers is automatically put in a more upright position, and can be held loosely, as well.

The paper should be held in place on the desk by the non-writing hand. That hand should be moving the paper about so the area of writing is just to the right of the body of the right-handed person, and just to the left of the left-handed person. In other words, the area of writing is always within the direct line of vision. The heel of the writing hand should not hold the paper in place. It should be free to glide along the line of writing. A restricted hand and wrist will cause tight, tense writing, concentrated in the fingers—*hand*writing will be ignored.

Most manuals give instructions for spacing. The BFH method of writing omits this instruction in the belief that posture, pen or pencil hold, and paper position, together with instruction in the rhythm of writing, govern spacing without ever mentioning the subject to students. See Section II.

It is often suggested to young children to put a finger down at the end of a word, then to write the next word on the other side of the finger. If one considers this idea, it could only apply to writing at the earliest stages. Even then it is counterproductive. Not only do little fingers grow, and some are quite large even in first grade, but as a child puts a finger in place to determine where to put the first letter of the next word, he or she is no longer using the non-writing hand to keep the paper in place, and the rhythm is interrupted.

This manual does not specify a slant for handwriting. The degree and direction of slant apparently is a characteristic of the handwriting of each individual, although it is largely influenced by the writer's posture and the position of the paper on the desk. The illustration on page six shows the proper placement of paper. If a student's writing slants excessively, check his or her posture, the position of the paper, and the pen or pencil hold. This last is often the culprit. When one's handwriting slants not in just one direction, but in several, the grip is too tight.

Writing that is straight up and down or which has only a slight forward slant is the most legible. Consider that almost all type used for text is vertical. Letters without any slant do not compress the counters (see Glossary) of letters. The open space inside letters is as significant to our ability to read as the dark lines that create letters. Most right-handers tend to slant their writing forward as they write rapidly. Too much slant will compress the counters and render them illegible. A slight forward slant is a happy compromise. The model alphabet for this manual has a slight forward slant, and its exemplars subtly set a standard.

A slight backslant, with clear letterforms is relatively easy to read, and it is often the preference of left-handers. If a left-handed student tends to have a "left hook", a wrist twisted to hold the writing instrument, it would be better for that student to undo the hook and write with a backslant, rather than suffer discomfort in later years when he or she has to write in that cramped position for an extended period of time.

A good writing surface can help anyone to write better. If a single sheet of paper rests on a hard surface, especially a desk on which someone has scratched into the surface, or has left the remains of a sticky snack, it is obvious that the writing instrument will have a bumpy ride. It is advisable to write on a pad of paper or to have a few sheets of paper stacked under the one to be used. Paper that is either bound in a workbook or in a loose-leaf binder is more difficult to write on than a pad or loose sheets, as the binding, or rings can interfere with positioning the hands.

It is easier to write on a slanted surface than on a flat one. Unfortunately, it is hard to find a desk with a slanted top. If a child has any visual problems that affect his or her writing, it is worth the trouble to provide a wedge that can sit on a desk or table top. See the illustration below, right. The wedge should be large enough to comfortably accommodate paper as it is moved into different positions for writing. It should have something, such as felt, glued to its bottom to inhibit slippage. Sometimes it is recommended that the student put the paper on top of a loose-leaf binder. However, if the paper is of the same size as that in the binder (and it most likely will be), the paper will be difficult to hold in position. Try it out, and you may find it even more awkward than the smaller illustration below indicates. Another solution is a lapboard. Any sturdy board, such as Masonite, will do. It should be a rectangle of about 16 by 20 inches, sufficient to rest in a student's lap at the point where the torso meets the legs, and against the edge of a desk or table.

A wedge placed on a desk or table.

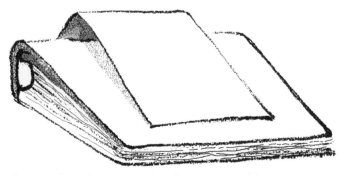
Paper placed on a notebook—an unstable arrangement.

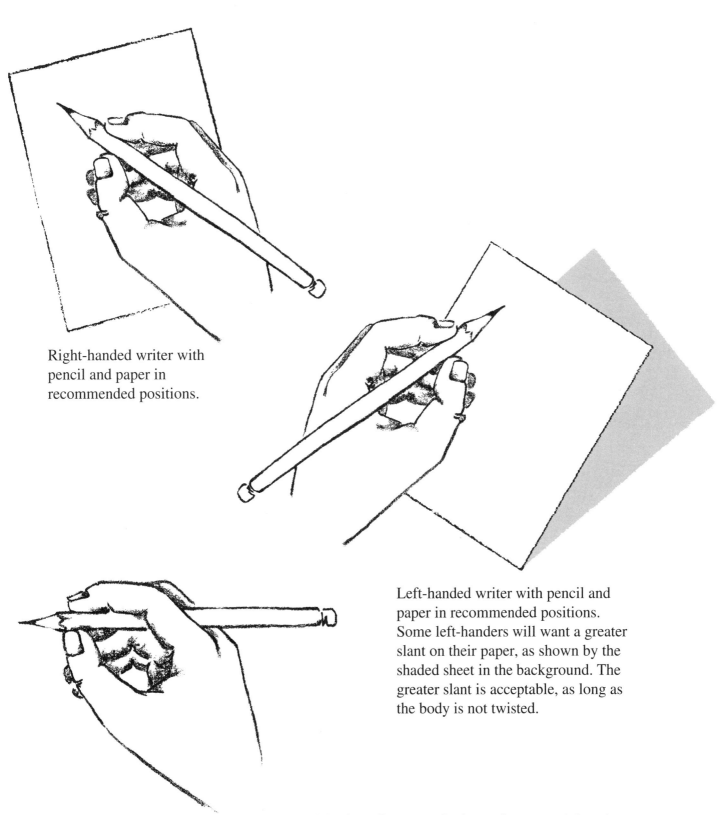

Right-handed writer with pencil and paper in recommended positions.

Left-handed writer with pencil and paper in recommended positions. Some left-handers will want a greater slant on their paper, as shown by the shaded sheet in the background. The greater slant is acceptable, as long as the body is not twisted.

An alternative pencil hold—especially good for long fingers or for loosening a too-tight grip. Left-handers may also choose this grip. Imagine the image reversed and the fingers moved back a little on the shaft of the writing instrument.

PAPER POSITION

- Right-handers should place the paper slightly to the right of the body. The paper position may vary slightly for right-handers. A variance is shown as a shadow on the example for left-handers.
- Left-handers should place the paper to the left of the body.
- Paper position should allow comfortable writing with a relaxed arm, wrist and hand. Left-handers should avoid a hooked wrist, or an elbow pulled too close to the body. Both postures are tiring.
- The ideal writing surface is a little softer than a bare desktop. Have a few extra sheets of paper as a cushion beneath the sheet being used. A 9 x 12 inch workbook works well as a cushion. It should not be a ring bound book; the rings get in the way.

SECTION II

rhythm

EXERCISE PATTERNS — **RELATED LETTERS & PRACTICE WORDS**

Exercise patterns directly relate to every aspect of fluent writing. *uuu* is the most basic and essential. It guides rhythmic movement in the proper directions. Rhythm controls spacing, and the slant, height, and size of letters. Each downstroke in the word *rhythm*, above, falls on a downstroke of the pattern in shadow. Exercise patterns should be used constantly as short, three-to-five-minute warmups at the beginning of each handwriting class. Choose the patterns from those listed herein that best fit the particular handwriting class. The patterns should also be used for remediation.

It is useful to play music during warmup time, or throughout the handwriting period. It is also a good idea to write the patterns with the eyes closed from time to time, in order to be fully aware of the *feel* of writing.

---

uuu uuu uuu uuu uuu uuu uuu uuu uuu

To write this pattern press gently on the downstroke and release on the upstroke. The purposes of the pattern are listed above. In addition, it relates to diagonal joins.

di nj up au iv aw ly

uuu uuu uuu uuu uuu uuu uuu uuu uuu uuu

This pattern provides practice for all of the letters in the *u* family. Please see Section III, pages 13-18.

uy adgq coe lt vw

Practice the letters with words like this:

cut way do let gave aqua cot cold

A join from the base line to *a, d, g, q, c* or *o* requires that the pen or pencil retrace the top of the letter. See Section VI. With good rhythm the retrace can be easily and clearly written. Avoid writing through letters like this: *a·d ccc ccc ccc ccc ccc ccc ccc ccc*

This pattern provides practice for the rhythm needed to join well with retraces. It is not as easy to write as some of the other patterns because it necessitates retracing at the top of the *c* s; however, it is excellent for helping those who tend to reverse the direction of *o*, and worth the extra effort to use it. Think of rolling waves on the ocean, and the practice will be more of a pleasure than a chore.

cage   age cot cold edge act mad

m m m m m m m m m m

This pattern provides practice for all of the letters in the *n* family. Please see Section III, pages 19-24.

nmrhk bp

Add a vowel and then practice words like this:

nip rim him kin bob hip rib

The retracing movement used for *cage* is the same as that used in joining from the bottom of *b* or *p*. Remember that joins should be made only when it is comfortable to do so. These retrace joins are not necessary. Avoid writing through letters like this: *bp*

Practice these words:

big pig past pin punk bumpy

nun unu nun unu nun

This pattern combines both clockwise and counterclockwise movement. Some practice words are:

unit unusual numb understand

sss sss sss sss sss sss sss

This pattern is not only useful for practicing s and its joining, but also helps to achieve the rhythm needed to join with retraces.

bag page   miss fussy boss bad
sassy pan cabbage Mississippi

join

Follow-through or flow is essential for rapid and legible writing. The pen or pencil should always move in and out of strokes with flowing motion. Just as one hits a ball, movement does not start and end with the impact; rather one moves before impact and follows through after impact.

rr rr rr rr rr rr rr rr rr rr rr

Practice r and its joining with words like this:

furry merry hurry strawberry

This pattern provides practice with spacing and rhythmic, flowing lift and replacement of the writing instrument. One instance when this movement is critical is for the two stroke p. The pattern looks like one long continuous line, however the movement is: *and down, bounce up and down to the descender line; lift the pen or pencil; replace it on the baseline, bounce up and down, bounce up and down to the descender line....*
Practice words follow.

nap nippy happy pump poppy

ullullullullullullullullu

This pattern is also good for spacing and rhythm. It helps the writer to avoid looping into ascenders, creating too much space between ascenders or shortening ascenders excessively. It is written: *and down, and down, and,* (here the pen or pencil may touch the next downstroke, but is lifted off the paper) *down, and lift, and down…*
Again, this pattern is not one long continuous line. Practice words follow:

lull lullaby hill baseball carefully

This pattern and the next two are to be written more as scribbles than as specific shapes. The one at the left should be used while the student focuses on posture and pen or pencil hold; there is no need to think about size or form. The focus gains greater impetus when the eyes are closed in both this one and the two patterns below, which are simply relaxing exercises that are especially good for students aged ten or older. The first of the patterns below moves counterclockwise and the other clockwise. Use whichever one applies best to a lesson. If written on lined paper, disregard the lines; the movement should be completely unrestricted.

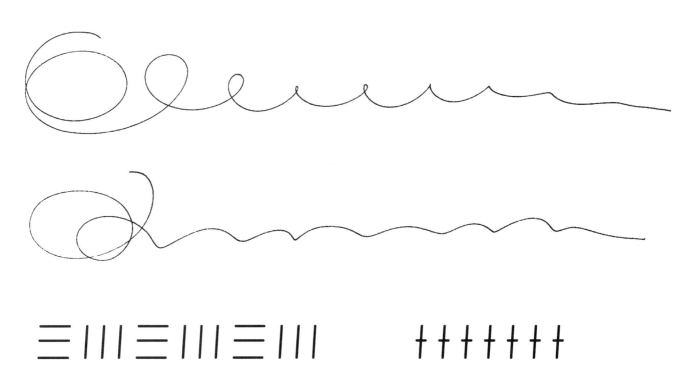

The last two patterns above help with the writing of capital letters. Please see Section IV for an explanation of their use.

REFERENCE FOR LOWERCASE ALPHABET

ARRANGEMENT BY SIMILARITY OF CONSTRUCTION; NONALPHABETICAL

When we read, we scan the tops of letters whenever possible. If a message is scrawled in a scramble of letters, we have two choices. We can attempt to decipher the mess, or trash it. The lowercase letters that follow are designed to be legible at scanning speed, as well as sympathetic to the natural, easy movement of the writer.

The letters are presented as belonging to families, rather than alphabetically. Most of the alphabet falls either into the *u* family or the *n* family, depending on whether the line that forms the body of the letter is written in a counterclockwise or clockwise direction. When working with any of the letters that fall into one of these two groups, please refer to the instructions for either *u* or *n*, as instructions for these parent letters will be the most complete. The exercise patterns, *uu* and *m*, are especially valuable for training small motor muscles to write letters rhythmically. Good rhythm in handwriting maintains legible letterforms and aids speed of writing.

Written *separately*, these lowercase letters will satisfy instructions that say, "please print." The very same letters will join for *cursive* writing. Please remember, the original meaning of "cursive," joined or running writing, is intended throughout this text, rather than the more common usage of the word, which refers to looped cursive writing.

The movement to form letters is constant and rhythmic. This makes handwriting fast, easy and accurate. The rhythm of writing will control both spacing and letter slant. Letter formation is simple for both the purposes of easy reading and easy writing. There are no loops in the models because beginning writers are discouraged from joining either into ascenders or from descenders. However, the BHF method of handwriting is flexible enough to allow older students to join to suit individual hands. If good writing habits of pen or pencil hold and movement are established early, legibility is not hampered significantly by altering the model. The letterforms of this alphabet depend upon pressure on the pen or pencil for the downstroke and definition of the letter, and a release of pressure for an upstroke within a letter and/or a diagonal join into a letter that follows. Please refer to Section I, page 2.

Spacing need not be taught. The space between downstrokes is usually very even, within letters, between them, and between words. Good spacing depends upon this sort of movement: *um*. Used as an exercise, this simple warmup pattern supports the movement needed to write well. It should be practiced frequently by young students in the many ways described in "Fast, Easy Handwriting for Beginners," found in the supplementary material on the CD-ROM, or in a separate, printed packet. Older students benefit by frequent, but short, practice periods.

The slant of letters is not mentioned in the instructions for the lowercase letters, nor in the instructions for capitals or numerals. Proper posture, placement of the paper, and pen or pencil hold will almost always yield a satisfactory slant, which will approximate the exemplars.

The small entry and exit strokes on some letters encourage the writer to join for cursive writing. Exit strokes are especially important. Strokes that end abruptly when they meet the baseline form habits of movement that directly oppose cursive writing. They lack the follow-through that enables the writing line to flow from letter to letter. Entry strokes are not so essential, although if omitted, some writers may tend not to join. It seems that if students learn to write letters without these strokes, they become satisfied with their success in forming legible letters, and then fear they may spoil the appearance of their writing with the addition of the serifs needed for joining. Or is it that habits become so ingrained that they are hard to change?

Some handwriting systems give almost as much instruction for the entry and exit strokes as for the letters themselves, and some, such as print-script (ball-and-stick), omit entries and exits altogether. Rhythmic movement is the name of the game. Consider these strokes only as the lead-in and follow-through that help to make the winning hit, be it for handwriting, baseball, tennis, or golf. The shapes of the entry and exit strokes are almost, but not quite, sharp. They are very slightly rounded to maintain fluid, rather than jerky movements.

Most of the letters in this section are illustrated with patterns to show the negative, or white spaces left by the writing lines. These areas are critical to legibility. Perhaps they would be better named "positive spaces." Negative spaces are similar in letters, and contribute to the ease with which they can be written. Please look at *u*, the first lowercase letter presented. The largest negative space, the counter, is shown by a slanted line pattern that is often repeated throughout this section. This is the most important shape to maintain. With *n*, the shape is simply turned upside down. A pattern of lines, slanted in the opposite direction, shows the triangular shape left by the writing line of *u* as it moves from the baseline to the midline. The lines might be thought of as secondary counters. The same shape, turned upside down again, is shown in *n*, where it is defined by the point at which the upstroke leaves the downstroke. Another pattern illustrates the space left by entry and exit strokes.

The direction of movement for constructing each letter is indicated by a thin line or lines with arrows. Almost every lowercase letter is written with just one stroke per letter. Whenever more than one stroke is needed, numerals at the starting points of the lines indicate stroke sequence.

Chants are suggested for beginning writers, and are shown in italics for each letter. Use them, or others that appeal to you and the students, to aid rhythmic writing, especially in the early grades. Saying, or singing what one is doing is great reinforcement. It is difficult to say, "down," and go up!

The instructions are specific. They may even seem, but are not intended to be, dogmatic. The intention is to provide a basic handwriting method, suitable for beginning writers, which will develop into a fast, legible, and personal hand. The older student will undoubtedly modify letter formation in later grades. "Rules are made to be broken." The breakage should be allowed or disallowed at the discretion of the sensitive, observant teacher. Individuality in the way one writes should be encouraged as much as what one writes; intelligibility forms the boundary lines in either case.

And down, bounce up, and down.
or: *And dive, swim up, and dive.*
(and add a soft flip as a reminder for the exit stroke),
After a very small lead-in movement, the writing instrument moves down to the base line, then directly up to the midline and down again with a small follow-through. The second downstroke retraces the upstroke to a point about halfway between the midline and the baseline. It is important to the rhythm of writing that the upstroke *bounces* right up to the midline rather than dragging along the baseline. The dragging movement is slow. Look at the lines that fill the counter, and at each of the other negative spaces. Look for similarities throughout this family of letters.

The letter u has within its family the letters y, a, d, g, q, c, o, e, l, t, v and w. All of the letters share a basic counterclockwise movement. The warmup pattern, uu, has the same movement as the letter u, and relates to the other letters in the u family. Although u is the head of the family, it need not be the first one taught. Letters should be introduced as needed for reading and writing.

u y a d g q

c o e l t v w

And dive, swim up, and dive to the bottom.
y moves in the exact same manner as u until the writing line reaches the baseline for the second time. Then its descender continues down in a clockwise direction. The length of the descender should equal no more than the body height of the letter.

Note the shape and size of the entry stroke, and the shape of the counter of y.

Over and down, and bounce, and down.
(Be sure the exit stroke is added.)
The line for a starts on the right side of the letter, moves over, curves a bit and then continues exactly like u.
Give a a nice broad top and a bouncing movement from the baseline to help it keep its shape. Note the little triangle that is like the one for u. This letter should be well rehearsed. It is one of the four letters most often misread; the others being r, t, and e.

Take care that the second downstroke goes all the way to the baseline. When joined, a could look like o: on

Note that the counter shape is clipped off on the upper left corner. A more angular a will read just as well: a

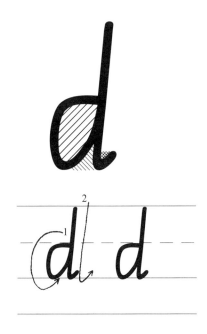

The little dog runs around, jumps up, and falls down.
To write d, begin as for a, to approximately this point:
where the writing instrument drifts off the paper.
Replace the pen or pencil on the ascender line and move
down. Practice of the uu pattern will establish the rhythmic, lifting motion needed to successfully write this letter
in two strokes. Some children will learn to write before
they achieve an adequate degree of small motor coordina-
tion, and for them d may be best written with one stroke.
The two stroke method of construction helps to keep d
together, preventing confusion with cl : cl, and avoiding a
loop in the ascender. Also, d will stay tall enough. If its
ascender becomes short, d will resemble a : a

*Gus, the gopher, runs around, jumps up, and goes down in
his hole to curl up.*
Again, begin as for a. When the pen or pencil touches the
baseline for the second time, it moves down as for y. Look
at the descenders and compare the shapes.

Over and down, bounce, down, and a little flip.
(Keep the voice low on the flip as a reminder that it is a
tiny mark.) Write q the same as g, with the exception that
the descender comes straight down, touches the descender
line, and then makes a slight flip up.

Note the shading at the end of q. The flip is the same shape
as the exit strokes, but it is not used for joining. If it were,
the line would travel so far to the u, which always follows
it, that the space between letters would be too great: *quiet*

If a student in later grades (four and up) uses the tail of q to
join to u successfully, it should be allowed.

III 15

Over and down and lift.
Move around for c, starting at the same point at which one would for a.

c, o, and e are usually grouped together. By teaching c first, and then o, the counterclockwise movement and the starting point for o are reinforced.

Over and down and around.
o starts at the same point as c, *not* at the middle of the top. Then it moves around as for c, but the line continues until it reaches its starting point. The o in the sample is neither a circle, nor an oval. The narrower bottom is caused by the bouncing movement off the baseline, an action which is rhythmic, not slowly drawn. The part of letters essential for reading is the upper half of the body of the letter, so it seems wise to take care with the tops and build speed in the lower parts of letters.

It is not always easy to see if a child has written o wrongly, from the bottom and around, and/or in a clockwise direction, unless the teacher observes the actual writing. Uncorrected, it will show up later and wreak havoc when o is joined to other letters. Establish counterclockwise direction with practice of this pattern: ccc ; the letters, c and o, and words that start with co, and are composed of letters in the u family.

cot coat cool cold

or: coat cool cold cocoa

Curl around and down.
e is the only letter in the alphabet which starts in its middle, not at the top. (It can be argued that d does not start at the top; however, if written with two strokes, each stroke starts at its top). Move up and around to the starting point of e and then finish as if writing c. It is *essential* that this letter be properly formed with an open counter. e is used most often; often it is abused. If it loses its counter, it loses its identity. e can look like an undotted i : ι, a poorly formed r : ι, or an l : ι . The word beet can look like but : but. Joining often obliterates the counter of e. Adequate time should be allotted for beginning writers to establish a habit of movement that will keep e strong under the duress of speed in later years. See Section IV, pages 48 and 49.

a, o, and e all need broad shoulders (tops) to keep them legible.

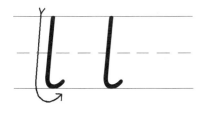

Down and out.
For l, move down from the ascender line to the baseline, curving the line a bit, as though writing the bottom of c, o, or e. Note that the counterclockwise movement at the end puts both l, and t in the u family, although both letters could just as well go into a separate "skinny" family with i, f, and j.

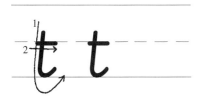

Down and out, and cross.
Write t, beginning just above the midline, so that its crossbar can be placed right on the midline. Come down just as for l, with the same curve at the baseline. As older students write t rapidly, the bottom of the letter may end abruptly at the baseline. That will happen because the writing instrument may move to the left and upwards to write the crossbar.

There is no designated line, such as ascender or midline, on first or second grade paper to show a starting point for t. Take care that beginning writers write it tall enough to allow for the crossbar, but not too tall. Some handwriting instruction shows t as tall as l. In almost all typefaces t is short—perhaps it looks better that way.

Please see Secvtion VI, pages 42 and 43, for the use of the crossbar for joining. This join can make a significant difference in the legibility of t, which is frequently hard to read.

And down and swing up.
v and w may be written with sharp turns at the baseline, or the turns may be rounded, as is the bottom of u. If movements are kept as consistent as possible, the rhythm is not changed as much with a rounded bottom, and one can write faster with accuracy.

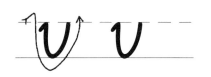

Start v as if writing u, stopping at the midline. It is essential that v swing in ever so slightly as it approaches the midline to allow it be legible when v joins to another letter. Don't overdo the swing, as the resulting line will be an excessive mark. See w.

To check up on letter similarity, try writing a v, and then write a u on top of it. The writing line of u will retrace the v very closely until the second downstroke of u is reached.

And down, up, down and swing up.
Start w as if writing v. When the midline is touched, come down as though writing another v with no space between them. It could well be called "double v" instead of "double u."

Please see the note on the swing-in at the end of v. Too often beginning writers produce something like the samples below for *vim* and *who*.

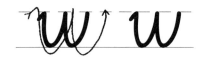

III 18

And down, bounce up and over and down.
After the lead-in or entry stroke, the writing instrument moves down to the base line, bounces up to the midline, over and down, and follows through with the exit stroke, which is just the same as the exit stroke for *u*. The upstroke should retrace part of the first downstroke, branching off about halfway between baseline and midline. The entry stroke is just *slightly* more round than that for *u*. The word, *slightly*, is stressed because excessively round entries can be misread as extra humps, causing *n* to look like *m*. The movement of the rounder entry serves in a subtle way as an introduction to the tops of the letters *n* and *m*, which must be rounded or these letters will be mistaken for *u* and *w*.

The letter *n* has within its family the letters *m*, *r*, *h*, *k*, *b*, and *p*. All of these letters share a basic clockwise movement. The warmup pattern, *m*, has the same movement as the letter *n* and is similar to that of other letters in the *n* family. As with *u*, *n* is the reference letter for a family, but need not be the first one of the group that is taught.

And down, bounce up and over and down, bounce up and over and down, and out.
The pen or pencil moves in exactly the same manner as it does for *n* until it reaches the baseline for the second time. Then it bounces up, and over, and down again.

n m r h k b p

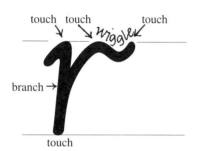

And touch the midline, down to the baseline, bounce up to touch the midline again, wiggle and touch again.
or: And touch, and down, touch, bounce up, touch, wiggle, touch.

The instructions for *r* are somewhat lengthy. This is another of the letters that is often misunderstood and needs extra instruction. Begin as for *n*, including the rounded entry, and continue until the writing instrument touches the midline for the third time. The rounded entry helps with the roll of *r* that comes before the wiggle. Note the word "branch" on the illustration. The point at which the upstroke moves away from the downstroke is critical to both legibility and ease of writing. The wiggle before the third midline touch allows *r* to join to letters legibly. Look at the shadings in the entry stroke, the triangle between the downstroke and the upstroke, and the shadow that represents the counter of *n*.

Here are some of the things that can go wrong:

1. The "arm" is too long. When another letter follows, the space between letters will be too great. The spacing between all downstrokes should be even, about equal to the "legs" of *n* for both ease of reading and speed of writing.

2. The upstroke did not touch the midline before wiggling.

3. The line has gone right through, and above the midline with almost no wiggle. Joining to a letter following *r* will not work.

4. An extra wiggle has been added. This shows a lack of understanding of how *r* should move.

5 & 6. The arm (the right extension of *r*) branches too low, causing *r* to look like *v*. The point at which the upstroke branches from the downstroke is very important in *r*. Better that it should branch too high than too low, although high branching is often a result of slow movement.

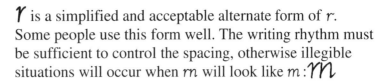 is a simplified and acceptable alternate form of *r*. Some people use this form well. The writing rhythm must be sufficient to control the spacing, otherwise illegible situations will occur when *m* will look like *m*:

Avoid joins from *r* to *e*. Please see Section VI, page 44.

Fall down, bounce up and over and down.
Begin at the ascender line to write *h*. Come straight down to the baseline and then finish writing *h* exactly like *n*.

Down, bounce up and over, tuck it in, and kick it out.
or: Down, jump up, and over. Get a pain in the tummy, grab it, and kick the pain away.
k is written exactly like *h* until the pen or pencil reaches the top, or arch. Then the line moves back to the downstroke, touching it halfway between midline and baseline; then it *kicks* out. The loop of *k* should not go above the midline, as it does in this sample:

The one-stroke method of writing *k* prevents something that looks like a capital (*K*) from appearing in the middle of a word, which happens all too often and gives the impression that the writer knows no better: *like*

It is helpful to teach *k* with capital *K* to make the differences more apparent. See Section IV, page 31.

Fall down, bounce up and over and tuck it in.
b is written like *h* until the pen or pencil moves over the arch and down toward the baseline, when it turns back to the downstroke.

Instruction of *b* and *p* as part of the *n* family helps prevent reversals of these letters. The bowls of both *b* and *p* move in a clockwise direction, and are on the right sides of the downstrokes.

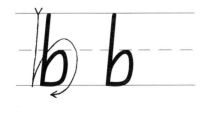

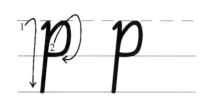

And down to the descender line. Lift. Back to the baseline, pop up and over and tuck it in.

The entry stroke for p is like that for u. The line moves down through the midline to the descender line, so there seems less need for a rounded entry to lead into the arch of p. For the second stroke the writing instrument is lifted, repositioned on the baseline, and then moves up along the first downstroke, pops over, and turns back to form a bowl exactly like the one on b. Good rhythm will allow the pen or pencil to move accurately and quickly to the baseline for the second stroke, and this two-stroke method will produce a cleaner looking p. However, if a child has undue difficulty controlling two strokes, allow him or her to write p with one stroke. The reasoning for two strokes is much the same as it is for d.

Turn this page upside down, go to page 15, and compare p with d.

If writing p with one stroke, do not let the lines separate, creating an open v shape: . The downstroke must be retraced up to the baseline.

Beginning writers often confuse lowercase p with capital P. It works best to teach both the lowercase and capital forms at the same time to help make the differences more evident. See Section IV, page 33.

And down and dot.
See the references to a "skinny" family under l.
i has entry and exit strokes like u. If one were to write the exercise pattern, uu, and put dots on it, it would be iii.

Often there is a tendency to put a circle on an i, rather than a quick and simple mark. Discourage circles, as they are time consuming. In the models you see here, the "dot" is really a tiny dash, which is an easier mark to make than a precise dot. Whether dot or dash, avoid excessive marks.

Swing over, get down and swing around.
s and f both move first in a counterclockwise direction and then in a clockwise direction. The top of s is written exactly like the top of a. Then the line swings down diagonally to the base line where it finishes with a movement similar to that of the bowl of b or p.

Please see Section VI, page 48, for the modifications that are made to s when it joins.

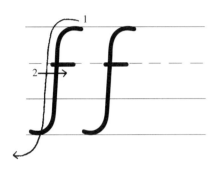

Over, straight down and swing; now back to the middle and cross.
The top of f is also written like a, but along the ascender line. Then it moves straight down to a point very near the descender line where it, like s, finishes with a shape similar to the bowls of b or p. The descender is the same shape as the descenders on g, j, and y. The shape and length of the descender is not critical. It may be easier for some students to eliminate the descender: f

If written as prescribed, f is the only letter with both an ascender and a descender. It is often troublesome, especially for some young hands that find it difficult to travel all the way from ascender line to descender line for just this one letter. That is why a shortened version should be allowed.

Here are some other things that can go wrong:

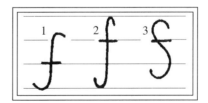

1. f has been started near the midline; therefore the tendency is to cross it on the baseline. The crossbar cannot then be used for joining. See Section VI, page 43.

2. f has a narrow top and bottom, indicating very restricted, tight movement.

3. The third *f* has a fiddle back. The line should move straight down. It is also too short, neither meeting the ascender nor the descender lines.

f may also be constructed in this manner:

And down and swing and dot.
The entry stroke for *j* is like that of *u* or *i*. Then the line moves straight down through the baseline, finishing at the descender line like *f*, or some of the other letters that have descenders.

As with *p*, lowercase *j* is often confused with capital *J*. Teaching them together helps to make the differences more evident. For some suggestions, see Section IV, page 30.

And slide down to the right. Go up and slide to cross.
"And" represents the entry stroke for *x*. The movement within the letter is easier if the entry is rounded like the entry for *n*, but the entry stroke is not essential. It appears to be larger than that of *n* because of the angle of the downstroke. The second stroke also starts at the top and moves diagonally to cross the first. This ductus for *x* provides the greatest consistency with the rest of the alphabet. The strokes move from top to bottom, and the first one goes left to right.

The exit stroke is there for the rhythm of movement; it cannot be used for joining because of the ductus.

Across, buzz back, and slide over.
Neither *x* nor *z* have the rhythmic movement of the rest of the lowercase alphabet. Fortunately, we do not write them often. Move from left to right along the midline for the width of *x* or *n* or *u*, then move diagonally to the baseline, and left to right again along the baseline.

REFERENCE FOR CAPITAL ALPHABET

Contrary to many opinions, capitals are not easier to learn than lowercase letters. They may or may not be easier to recognize, but they are more difficult and time consuming to write. Take a moment and a scrap of paper to test this premise. Close your eyes to best concentrate on your movements. Write an A and then an a. Repeat the writing and consider the number of times the pencil must be lifted for each, the distance the pen or pencil must travel and the flow of the movement. Even if you write an *a*, there is still more distance to go for the capital than for the lowercase letter. Uncertain? Try other comparisons.

The capitals, as presented in the exemplars, and as typed out with Barchowsky™ Fluent Hand™, are Spartan. They resemble a sans serif type: *ABCDE*. Students will quite naturally flourish the capitals a little as their handwriting matures and flows more freely. The results may resemble this: *A B C D E*, but there is no need to teach anything other than the basic forms. The students' flourishing should not become excessive, affecting legibility or speed. Alternate forms are shown for some of the letters, with explanations.

The instructions for writing each stroke of each letter follow the rule of moving from top to bottom and left to right, with no exceptions. If teachers of young children require that their students follow the specific ductus shown for each capital letter, the letters will retain a clearer, stronger shape as the students grow older, develop their own styles, and write faster. The specified ductus should be maintained until children are at least eight or nine years old.

Instructions for most looped cursive capitals require the writer to change the directions of writing lines frequently. These capitals are rarely seen in type. In actual use, they are frequently illegible and certainly not speedy. The only reason they are often taught is that they have become a familiar tradition to many people. The BFH capitals are also based upon a tradition, an older and stronger one.

The capital letters are presented in alphabetical order. Unfortunately, neither capitals nor numerals are as easy to group into characters of similar movement as the lowercase letters. Fortunately, capitals are not needed as often as lowercase letters. Throughout this section there are notations of the similarities between various capital letters which suggest ways to group them to make instruction easier.

The height of capitals is often shown to be equal to the height of ascenders. In this manual capitals are shown just a little shorter, partly for aesthetic reasons and partly because of legibility. The construction of capital letters causes them to take up more space than lowercase letters, for example; B is bigger than b, **B** is bigger than **b**, L is wider than l, and **L** is wider than **l**. Therefore, when capitals are written shorter than lowercase letters, they are in a more agreeable proportion with each other. When capitals are larger, they tend to stand out too much on a page of text, and distract the reader's eye.

There are two good warmup exercises to use with lessons on capitals. The first is:

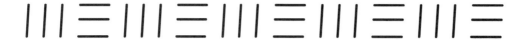

Chant for or with the children, *Down, and down, and down, across, and across, and across...* Each stroke reinforces top-to-bottom or left-to-right movement. Practice of the direction and control of the lines prepares children to write A, E, H, and all the other capitals that are composed of straight lines. The downstrokes will be easy, although the spacing between them may be less than perfect. Poor spacing in the pattern is unlikely to adversely affect spacing when writing the letters, so it can be overlooked here.

Watch the students as they write. Some children may shift the paper, thinking that it might be easier to make the horizontal lines look like the downstrokes. Some may twist their hands and wrists to make the downstrokes. Others may write these lines from right to left, especially left-handers. Right-to-left lines in the exercise or for crossbars of letters interrupt the flow of writing, so ***proper practice is important***. The direction in which a mark is made on a finished paper is often difficult to detect, so one must observe the act of writing.

Many capitals have crossbars near their centers: A, E, H, etc. Others, such as B, K, etc., have a second stroke that moves back to touch the first at its center. The second exercise helps students to write these letters.

Chant for or with the children, *down, mark it, down, mark it...*
Write a downstroke, then put a small mark at the point that seems to be the center of the line. The chanting will discourage students from writing a series of vertical strokes and then going back to make the marks.

The flaw in teaching capitals at a shorter height is that children tend to follow the guidelines on their paper. For capitals they must ignore both the ascender line and the midline. Some teachers may prefer to teach larger capitals, and some may teach capitals on unlined paper. If students are learning to write them on lined paper, as this manual suggests, some extra instruction is needed to make children aware of the visual center of the letter. The bit of extra effort is worthwhile.

Slide down a mountain; ski down the other side; go through the tunnel.
Start at the top, and come down to the baseline at an angle. Lift the pen or pencil, go back to the top, and come down the right side, moving toward the right. Now lift the pen or pencil, and put it halfway down the first stroke. Move across from left to right. The crossbar should appear to divide the tent of A in two equal parts, which puts it lower than the crossbar of any other capital letter. Even if A is as tall as the ascender line, the crossbar will make an awkward looking division if placed at the midline: A

Capitals do not have as much fluency as lowercase letters, but there is some. Note the flow of the writing instrument as it moves on and off the paper, as indicated by the dotted lines through the grayed A.

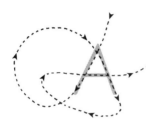

Older students may write a satisfactory A with two strokes, moving from the baseline on the left to the top of the letter, and then down on the right, then adding the crossbar. Also an A may evolve into a one stroke letter, with the line drifting on the paper from the lower right-hand corner of A to make the crossbar.

An alternate form of A may be an enlargement of the lowercase letter a . A is presented in this manual as the preferred form because it is distinct in its shape from the lowercase form, and because it resembles the A found in most printed text.

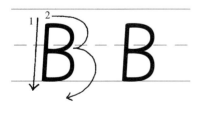

Put a stick in the ground. Bounce around and around.
This two-stroke letter can be grouped with others that are made up of one vertical stroke and a second that is a semicircle and/or meets the first at its center: D, K, P, and R. After writing the downstroke of B, lift the pen or pencil and replace it at the beginning of that stroke to write two semicircles. Think of writing around two half moons, two halves of an orange, or even a hamburger cut in two. Beginning students will seldom write B with nicely sized bowls. The ability to write this letter, or other capitals, with good proportions will come with time, small motor development, and practice.

The B, as just described, seems most likely to succeed in retaining legibility. If written with one stroke, starting at the top, going to the baseline, and back up to write the bowls, either of the two following samples may evolve. Neither is quite as clear as a B written with two strokes. The first sample has a distracting loop; the open v-shaped space in the second one makes it hard to read.

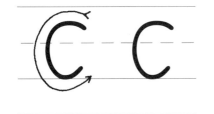

Over, down and around, and lift.
C has the same shape and movement as c, only it is larger. Give both a generous right-to-left movement at the top to maintain their legibility. If taught before O, the counter-clockwise movement is established, just as it is with the lowercase forms. If you are grouping the rounded letters together, think of C as having its mouth open; O's is closed, G is sticking its tongue out, and Q closed its mouth, but forgot to pull in its tongue.

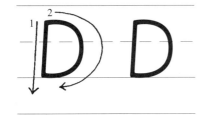

Come on down. Back up and bounce around.
The letter D relates well to B. Write a downstroke. Go back to the top of that stroke, and swing a second stroke out, and around, and back at the baseline. If you wrote around two halves of an orange for B, this time it can be one grapefruit half. Then the bowl of P can be referred to as one large orange half. Finish an orange half for R and throw it away. Kick all the fruit at the stick for K and it bounces off.

It is better to avoid D with only one stroke. D can lose its legibility in the same way as B:

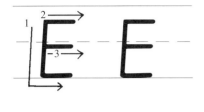

Fall down. Slide to the side. That's an L*! Now hop on top and make it an* E*: write to the right, and write to the right.*
If it fits the language arts program, it is easiest to teach I first, then L, and then E. A straight line comes down for I. For L the line takes a turn at the baseline and moves to the right, with no lift of the writing instrument. For E lift the pen or pencil after writing an L shape, go back to the starting point, and write a horizontal line to the right. Again lift the pen or pencil, go to the middle of the first downstroke, and write another line from left to right.

Ɛ is perhaps an easier form to write, as it has only one stroke. It was not selected for this manual because of its dissimilarity to capitals found in printed text. Allow older students to write Ɛ if they wish to do so.

Fall to the floor; to the top for more. Now write to the right and right again.
F relates well to E. It is just the same, except that the first stroke is I instead of an L.

Over, down and around and lift. That's C.
Its tongue hangs down and makes a Ꝿ.
Write a C, but keep the writing instrument on the paper to move down and write a short tail. The tail should stop about halfway between the baseline and the descender line. Take care that the tail does not grow so long that it wraps around the descender line. A tail may end at the baseline.

G is a good form of Ꝿ, but it is not so easy to teach and maintain. It should be written with two strokes; first write a C. Lift and replace the pen or pencil inside the counter and move right and down. Unfortunately, many students do not control the second stroke well and write it as though drawing a chimney or a shelf: G̚

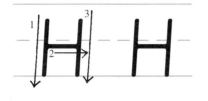
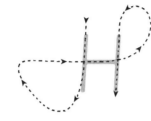

Hang down. Hop to the middle and hike to the right. Hang down over there.

First write the downstroke on the left, then the crossbar (of course it goes left to right), and then the downstroke on the right. This is the ductus that is recommended for writing H. It is the shortest route for the pen or pencil to take. It seems to control the size of the letter and the positioning of the strokes best, perhaps because of the flow of the writing instrument, indicated by the dotted lines. The two downstrokes can be written first with the crossbar written last if that seems more comfortable.

Just drop to the baseline.

This letter is just one simple downstroke. Serifs are often put on I and J: I J. Exemplars in this manual leave them off to be consistent; no other capital letters in BFH have serifs. It is worth noting that I looks like the numeral 1, and for that reason you may want to add serifs, or inform students in later grades that they may encounter the letter with the numeral, in an address code for example, and a differentiation must be made. The same problem exists for the letter O, and the numeral O. See Section V, page 38, for some suggestions.

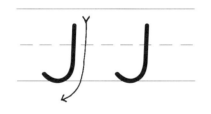

Just hang from Never, Never Land and swing to the left.
J moves just like I, but it curls at the baseline. Beginning writers often have trouble distinguishing the capital J from the lowercase j. It seems best to teach, or review j when teaching J to make the different placements on the guidelines more obvious.

For practice, use short sentences such as:

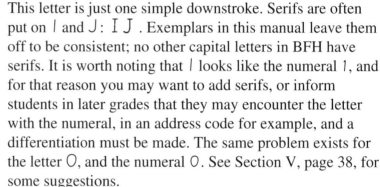

IV 30

A little of the history of our language can enhance handwriting instruction for older students, especially if European history is part of the curriculum. Most of our capital alphabet is more than two thousand years old. It comes from the Roman Empire; the language that Romans spoke and wrote was Latin. Most Spanish, French, and Italian words come from Latin ones, as do many English words. K existed before the Roman Empire, but the Romans did not use it. It was revived in the Middle Ages, sometime between 800 and 1300 AD. In the Middle Ages, V was often written so it looked like U. Later, they became separate letters. J and W have been in our alphabet for only about 400 years.

The Romans wrote cursively, but the lowercase alphabet as we know it began to develop about 1,300 years ago.

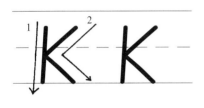

Put a stick in the ground. Go to the top, then back to the stick. Kick the stick and hike away.
Write K with just two strokes: first a downstroke, and then a second stroke which starts over to the right, comes back to its first stroke, and then kicks out. Some instructions call for the second stroke to stop when it touches the first stroke; then a third stroke starts at a point on the second stroke, just to the right of the first stroke to finish the letter. That construction is unnecessarily complicated and is no more legible than the two-stroke K.

Refer to the instructions for J and P. By teaching students to write k with one stroke, you will circumvent the confusion that is common between K and k.

For practice, use short sentences such as:

Kangaroos kick.
Kate likes (licks) the cake!
Kira has a koala.
Keith likes to fly kites.

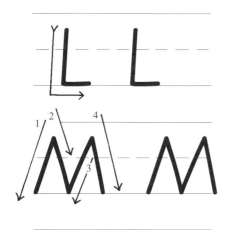

Fall down. Slide to the side.
As described for E, a straight line comes down as for I, and the line takes a turn at the baseline and moves to the right, all in one stroke.

Down one. Slide to the side for two. Slide to meet two, and down again for four.
M is another letter that must be taught carefully, and watched after it is first taught. If it is written with four downstrokes, its shape will remain intact. By teaching students the four-stroke method, you are also teaching control of letter shapes, and consistent direction.

Some students may not bring the second and third strokes all the way to the baseline, which is not so important, as long as four downstrokes are used until students attain fluency. Older, more fluent students may modify the number of strokes. Just beware of something that looks like this: . Distortion is often the result if one downstroke is written on the left, and the letter is completed with a second stoke that moves down, and up, and down.

There are some tricky, calligraphic aspects of M that the teacher may want to understand, although there is no need to burden students with this information. The lines of the exemplar M create three equal counter shapes with its slanted sides. None of these lines is parallel (the lines that form W are parallel.) The equal counter shapes give M maximum legibility, but if students do not write M exactly like the exemplar, it is not important.

Fall down one, slide over two, and fall for three.
As with M, there is a temptation to write N with just one or two strokes. N will lose its shape unless written with three strokes. If written with two strokes or one, which starts at the baseline, it may look like this: . Worse, and a too common error, the diagonal stroke may go wrong if N is written with one stroke, starting at the top: . Again, control of the hand and the writing instrument is important training.

Both N and M are often presented as enlarged forms of the lowercase letters. The reason for the forms of N and M are the same as for the form of A.

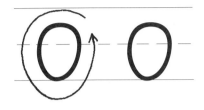

Over and down and around.
Practice of C before O will help reinforce counterclockwise direction, just as it does for the lowercase forms of these letters. The capital letters C, O, S, and Z are all written exactly like c, o, s, and z. They are just larger.

Put a stick in the ground. Bounce around.
Just as with D, write a downstroke, go back to the top and add one semicircle, except this semicircle is smaller and meets the first stroke near its middle. The meeting point is just below that for B or R, but no mention of this is necessary. As long as the construction is correct, the proportion of the letter will usually fall into place.
If it does not, no legibility is lost.

Many children have difficulty distinguishing between P and p, just as they do with J and j. The letters look just enough alike to be confusing, and beginning writers are dealing with a variety of instructions all at once. They should learn to write both P and p with two strokes, put the letters in their proper places on the guidelines, and make the strokes just a little different. Perhaps children are even wondering why they need both P and p! Teaching capital P with a review of p makes the distinctions much easier for the students.

Sentences to practice can include:

Peter is a piper.

Pepe likes peppers.

Pat has a pink pig.

Avoid writing either P or R with one stroke, for the same reason as that given for B and D:

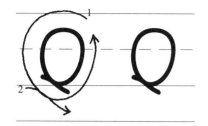

All around on the Q trail.
This quirky letter needs a tail.
Q is written with two strokes. Write O. Lift the pen or pencil and replace it on the left and near the baseline. Make a small mark, again moving from top to bottom and left to right. The small second stroke must touch the first. It may just touch as in Barchowsky™ Fluent Hand™, or the tail may start inside the counter and move to the outside: Q

Q may also be written by first making half of an O, lifting the pen or pencil near the baseline, and replacing it at the starting point. Then the second half of the O is made, and the line continues to change the O to a Q by adding a tail. The Q written by the last method should look almost like the BFH model: Q .

When children are taught to write Q in this last manner, they often are tempted to make excessive curls at its bottom, so the first two methods are preferred.

Q is used much less frequently than other capitals. Be aware that children can forget how to write it, so its construction needs to be reviewed occasionally throughout elementary grades.

Rest a stick in the ground. Bounce around and kick it down.
Write a downstroke and add a semicircle as for P, and then finish it with a kick out as if finishing the second stroke of K. For the same reason as given for K, a two-stroke method of writing R is best.

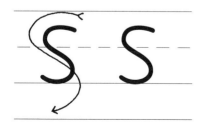

Swing over, and swing around.
S shares a swing with its smaller sister.

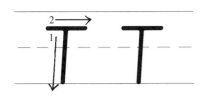

Throw a hat to the ground, nice and light. Pick it up and toss it to the right. Or, if the stroke order is reversed: *Run to the right. Drop to the ground.*
Write a straight line down and then put the crossbar on the top, or reverse the ductus if you wish. The important thing to watch for is a crossbar written left to right.

Down, swing up, and come on down.
Start at the top and left, as always, and move down and around and up and back down to the baseline, as though writing a large lowercase u. Older students will probably add small serifs as they gain fluency, in which case U, V, W, and X will all look like enlarged lowercase letters:

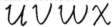

Be sure that students complete U by writing the last downstroke. Sometimes it is omitted, and a handwritten U can be confused with V.

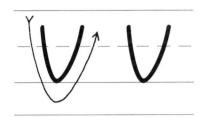

Down, swing up.
Again, this letter is written just like its lowercase counterpart, but it may be better to teach it without an entry stroke for beginning writers.

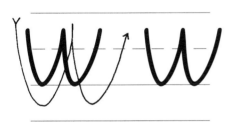

Down, swing up; down, swing up.
Please go back to page 32 and have another look at M. W looks almost like an upside down M; yet, W can be written with just one stroke with no danger of distortion. The reason is in a subtle difference in seemingly parallel strokes—no need for an explanation to students, but the instructor may want to know. Neither the first and third strokes of M, nor the second and fourth strokes are parallel. With W, whether the strokes are curved or straight, these same strokes are parallel, or nearly so.

W, too, is like its lowercase counterpart, but without an entry stroke. However, as with U and V, there is never anything wrong with a little flow into a letter.

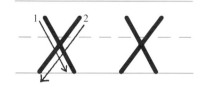

Slide down to the right. Go to the top, slide across.
Be certain to follow the same ductus used for x. It is consistent with the direction prescribed for all capitals. Small serifs can be added to the first stroke.

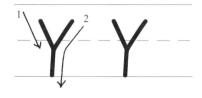

Slide to the right; stop at the middle. Go to the right, slide to the middle, and come on down. Why? To write Y.
Write the first stroke of Y by moving at a slant from the top of the letter down to about where the center of the letter will be. (Remember to ignore the midline on the writing paper.) Start the second stroke over to the right, and move at a slant to make the second stroke meet the end of the first, but don't lift the pen or pencil; just make a little turn and move to the baseline. It might help to think of an upside down ice cream cone stuck on a stick, or maybe a student might have another idea of what Y resembles.

Buzz to the right, slide down, and buzz to the right.
This is just a big z.

SECTION V

REFERENCE FOR NUMERALS

Numerals are easiest to learn when grouped according to their ductus. The movements that compose the numerals are less rhythmic than those that create the lowercase letters. Many children are confused about where to start and where to go with their pens or pencils. However, sometimes it is necessary to teach numerals in their usual sequence.

7, and some of the other numbers, are prone to reversal. If 7 is taught with 2 and 3, the direction of the first movement is easier to remember. Put 1, 4, and 5 together; they all start with a downstroke. 6 can also go with these, or be grouped with the rounder numerals that swing over toward the left: 0, 8, and 9.

As with both lowercase letters and capitals, the movement and shape of the numerals is reinforced by large motor activities. For example, for 7, ask children to point to something in the classroom (a window, perhaps), then ask them to swing their arms over to another reference point (a picture on the wall), and then point to the floor.

Chanted directions are helpful. Use the ones suggested with each numeral, or make up a chant that you like better, or take a cue from a student. If an idea comes from one of the children, it will make a much stronger impression on all of the class.

No warmup pattern for numerals relates well to more than one or two numerals, because the movement differs for each one. Placement of numerals is critical. A crooked column of figures is hard to add. Practicing the following pattern will help. The slant is unimportant as long as it is consistent, but emphasize spacing, and its dependence on the rhythmic movements learned in other patterns, and in lowercase letters.

The numerals, as they appear in the Barchowsky™ Fluent Hand™ font, are just a little shorter than capitals. They can be as tall as capitals or even shorter than the samples; their height is not critical. However numerals must be similar in size.

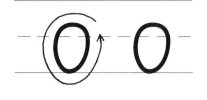

Go around a hole where there is nothing at all.
or: *Run around the sun.*
The directions for writing 0 are the same as for writing o or O. 0 starts at the point where one would start c or o; then it moves over, around and down to the baseline. It bounces off the baseline and moves back to its starting point. The shape is just slightly smaller and narrower than O.

Sometimes legibility is especially important. For example, some foreign address codes are a mixture of numbers and letters. To distinguish between 0 and O, zero can be shown this way: Ø (Type shift option o). Alternate forms of numerals are not needed for beginning writers, but they can be introduced to older students. See 1 and 7.

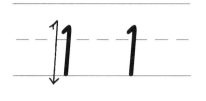

Down one just for fun.
or: *One is fun. Once down and it is done.*
One simple stroke down is all that is needed for 1.

1 closely resembles l, especially in the Barchowsky™ Fluent Hand™ font. There is just a small serif at the top of 1.

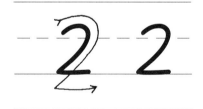

Two is a hook, and a slide to the side.
or: *Around and back on a railroad track.*
Move over to the right, and around, and down to the baseline. Finish 2 with a line along the baseline that moves to the right. Avoid excessive curves and curls, although the movement is freer if the last part is just slightly curved.

Side step, slide, and around for three.
or: *Flat top, slide down, and run around.*
Move from left to right, come down at an angle on the left and then swing around. Compare the bowls of both 3 and 5 to the bottom bowl of B. The first part of 3 is exactly like the first part of 7, unless 3 is written with a rounded top: 3. Either 3 is acceptable, but if you use the one with the curved top, group it with 2.

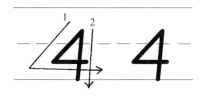

Slide on down, but not too far. Fly to the right. Climb to the roof and fall to the floor.
or: *Slide down, run to the store; back to the top and fall to the floor.*
4 and 5 are the only numerals that require two strokes. Move down, take a sharp turn, and go to the right. Now go back to the starting point, and write a downstroke, which must cross the last part of the first stroke. 4 can also be written this way: 4.

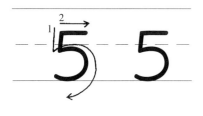

Ski down and round the tree that's fat. Go back up to put on your hat.
Move down almost halfway to the baseline, then swing around. This part is like the bottom bowl of B. Then go back and add the top stroke that goes from left to right. It is important that children form the habit of writing 5 with two strokes. Sometimes it is written with just one, and the result looks like S. Teach 5 with 1 and 4 to help students write 5 clearly.

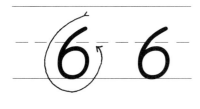

Slip down six and curl it up.
or: *Down and around and lock it when you land.*
If convenient, teach 6 with 0. Curl the line down to the baseline, and then come around to make a circle at the bottom.

Run on top. Slide to drop.
or: *What walks to the right and slides to the left?*
Teach 7 with 2 and 3. Move along the top and then come to the baseline at a slant to the left.

Some people put a slash through 7 like this: 7. Then if the top is short, it will not look like the numeral 1.

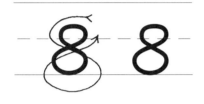

Take the train to the left, swing south and around. Cross the track and run back to town.
or: *Follow the track; swing to the south, swing around. Cross your path and you are back up north.*
These instructions, and many of the others, reinforce direction. Begin 8 as though writing S, by moving in a curve to the left and then swinging around and down to the baseline. Continue the line all the way back to the beginning.

Some students make an 8 with two circles, one on top of the other, an inefficient formation. Discourage it.

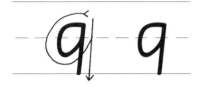

Around a rotten apple; hang it on a stick.
Move over to the left and around to the starting point. Then go straight down to the baseline. Why a rotten apple? The first part of 9 is a droopy circle, like fruit that has rotted and become soft, or a balloon that you blew up yesterday. Compare the counter to that of a. Why a "droop"? If the term is displeasing use another, but focus on forming the numeral quickly and easily. The writing line moves over to a point where the counter can be clearly defined, then down, and directly up to write the downstroke.

9 can also be written this way: 9. It looks like the one in the type you are reading (9). The first version probably is the more efficient. This second version must be written with two strokes: Come around from the top as if to write a c, and then go back to the beginning of the c shape to finish with a curved downstroke.

JOINING LETTERS

The ligatures of letters are presented in the order in which it is suggested that they be taught. They are arranged according to ease of joining and the effect upon letter shapes, all of which are better explained with the specific instructions that follow. Note that the order is *suggested*. It can be changed at the teacher's discretion. It is wise to teach all joins at the earliest possible level. As students learn to master joining in the early grades, they are learning to control letter shapes, and they are establishing habits of movement that sustain those shapes in later years when academic pressures intensify. The joins that are most critical to legibility are items one through five, ten, and eleven.

In these instructions "ligature" or "join" indicates that the writing instrument remains on the paper between letters, making one continuous line. The usage here is skewed a bit, because the dictionary does not give quite the same definitions for either "ligature" or "join."

The BFH method of handwriting requires that letters be joined only if there is an easy, natural flow from letter to letter. Looped cursive methods require that every letter in every word be joined, even though some of the joins involve movements that must be made slowly to avoid distortion of letters. Handwriting can be more speedy if the need to join supports, rather than interferes with the writer's ease of letter formation.

The goal for handwriting is maximum legibility with maximum speed.

In order to achieve this goal, teachers must understand the instruction for not only the grade level(s) for which they are responsible, but for the grades and years that follow. These instructions are directed primarily to beginning writers. They also include some of the modifications that can be made as students grow and develop.

Students who have already learned to write a looped cursive hand may be joining all letters within words, or they may have reverted to the print-script that they learned early on. For students who have illegible handwriting, modifying the requirement to always join may improve their handwriting by helping them to relax. They will write more rhythmically, with the results that the letters will become more uniform in size and slant, the writing will stay on the baseline, and tangling of descenders and ascenders will be relieved.

Students who first learned print-script, then looped cursive, and who have reverted to print script, can make a few adjustments to their handwriting to achieve cursive, or joined handwriting, which moves more fluently and has a more adult appearance. Section III will provide help for these students. Also refer to section VII.

Beginning writers will learn to write their names first. If the child's name is *Patricia*, *Alfred*, or *Marty* teach him or her to use the crossbar of *f* or *t*, and the arm of *r* for joining from the very beginning. This instruction may seem difficult, but it is certainly no more difficult than learning to put three separate strokes in the right places to form A, and the end results will prevent some legibility problems when the student writes rapidly.

1. *Always* use the crossbars of *f* and *t* when a horizontal join can be made. These joins help to keep the crossbars in place, and they control the heights of the letters that follow the crossbars. *t* is one of four letters in the alphabet that most often is illegible; the crossbar often misses its mark, as in **tile**, *tile*. (According to Barbara Getty and Inga Dubay, authors of several books on handwriting, the most illegible letters are all found in the word **rate**.)

Note that the entry strokes on letters that follow *f* and *t* are eliminated.

Examples, with some letters omitted as unlikely combinations with *f* or *t* :

fi ti fm tm fn tn tp fr tr

fu tu tv tw fy ty

Words to practice: *fun fine free tie Batman tree tug party outpost*

Practice any sentences with words that use joins that relate to those just described. For example, the sentences shown in this section use joins from *f* and *t*. The sentences are suggestions only. Change them to suit the interests of students, or let students create their own sentences. They will enjoy the lesson more. Some of the longer sentences are suggestions for students that need remediation. Few make sense. Maybe silly ones work better.

If a name is used in a sentence, and a student has a name with the same joins, substitute that name.

Suggested sentences:

Goofy fish fry in the city.
The fierce tide tumbled on the shore in misty, twisty twirls.

Cross *ff*, *tt*, *ft*, and *tf* with one stroke only, writing the two downstrokes first. Should *i*, *y*, or another letter follow, which can be joined horizontally, the pen or pencil should remain on the paper from the beginning of the crossbar to the end of the letter. These joins avoid awkward meetings of lines. The first sample below, looks smoother than the second; the second could look even worse!

crafty   crafty

Examples:

ff tt ft tf

Words and suggested sentences to practice: *fluffy kitten raft hatful*

Sift the glitter for some nifty stuff.

Send a little letter to the catfish.

Joins from crossbars into *e* frequently cause distortion to that letter. Such joins should be disallowed, especially in the early grades. Older students may be allowed to use these joins if they do so without undue distortion. Here are some of the distortions that can occur: *fe te ft tt ft tt*

It is advisable not to join from the baseline of *t* to *e*, because to make the join, one must change the order of strokes from those that are used for other joins from *t*, which move horizontally at the midline, and encourage immediate crossing of the *t*. Habits of consistent movement promote fast and legible writing.

Words and suggested sentences to practice: *feel fence ten tent after*

I feel fine.

Often Steve finds ten tins of steamed fish feasts.

Joins from crossbars to ascenders should not be taught to beginning writers. See page 50, Exceptions. Fluent writers will join *the* something like this: *the*, which is permissible.

2. *Always* join from *r* when a horizontal join can be made. Note the elimination of entry strokes, as in item 1. The previous comments on discouraging joins from crossbars to *e* also apply to joins from the arm of *r*. The results can be:

re rl rt rc

Please see Section III, pages 20 and 21.

Examples:

ri rm rn rp rr ru ry

Here are words and suggested sentences to practice that include combinations of letters that are similar, but follow different rules. Instruction will be reinforced.

ride harm barn harp run try berry

The red river runs dry.

Harry charmed a gorilla by strumming his harp.

The terrible tiger trembled.

Remember that when two *r*s are followed by *i* or *y*, the writing line continues from the first *r* to the end of *i* or *y*.

Please note that it appears that *r* can touch *f* or *t* in exemplars, but there is no join to *f*; a join would be a convoluted maneuver. *t* is short so the arm of *r* can easily move into the downstroke of *t*. Please see section VIII, page 64. To teach this join, one can use something from a supplement, make up an exemplar or demonstrate on the chalkboard.

3. Always join diagonally unless too many diagonal joins follow in succession. The rule for beginning writers should be, join no more than three to five letters. It is obviously quicker to leave the writing instrument on the paper between letters such as *i* and *n* than it is to lift it and then reposition it.

It is easier to write: *minimum*, than *minimum*.

This rule can be relaxed when students achieve fluent writing.

Examples of diagonal joins:

mi nj up nu iv mu uy

t is short enough to be included in this group: *it*

Words and suggested sentences to practice: mile enjoy pup numb ivy nut any nip mud buy little bit nut butter

Smile at mice.

A pup nips at a nut with butter on it.

A diagonal join can move out from any letter with an exit stroke at the baseline.

Examples:

ai di hi ii ki mi ni ui

The lines that form c, e, and z may be continued into the next letter.

Examples:

ci ei zi

For diagonal joins from *b*, *p*, and *s*, see item 9.

4. This category is separated from the last one for those who teach a rounded entry for *n*, *m*, *r*, and *x*. Otherwise, items 3 and 4 may be combined. Refer to the *n* family, Section III, page 19. Note that the entries to *n*, *m*, *r*, and *x*, as typed, are just very slightly rounded.

Examples:

um un ur ux

Words and suggested sentences to practice: am any ham Danny arm are ax

Dan is slim.

Swim under and around the ample arena.

5. Always join horizontally into letters that require no retracing, unless too many joins follow in succession. When joining from *v* or *w*, the need for the slight swing inward for the upstroke becomes obvious. It should be *ivy* not *ivy*, and *win*, not *win*.

Examples:

vi on op wr ow om ox

Words and suggested sentences to practice: *vim on open write over cow ox*

Cows visit some oxen.

Don't write over your own words.

6. Join horizontally to those letters that require retracing. The pen or pencil retraces, moving forward and back where the solid line appears in the illustration. It is useful to teach students to join horizontally into letters that require retracing as soon as possible. They may or may not choose to use these joins later on, but the instruction will reinforce good letter formation of those letters into which the joins are made. Broad tops on *a, d, g, q, o,* and *s* help to keep these letters legible.

Examples:

ta oc od og to oq ts

Words and suggested sentences to practice: *tan ocean odor toad tots*

Is your coat cozy?

A tiny toad is lost in the fog.

A cowboy cooks cookies for a tortoise.

7. The wiggle in *r*, which is necessary for it to join legibly, makes the join to letters that need retracing more difficult. It can be taught to beginning writers for the same reason as that given in item 6. Instruction of this join is not required. In the first four typed examples that follow, *r* almost touches, but the writing line does not actually flow into the following letter. (For an explanation of the font restrictions, see Section VIII, page 64.) For the next four examples, the letters have been typed, then retouched. To teach this join, one can use something from the lesson plans in a supplement, make up an exemplar or demonstrate on the chalkboard.

Examples:

ra rc ro rs   ra rc ro rs

Words and suggested sentences to practice: ran arc road cars barge

March on the road.

Carol ran around a rose colored rabbit.

The brown dog was drowsing on the barge.

8. Good writing rhythm prevents the writing line from crossing through the counters of letters when joining diagonally; however, it is well to teach these joins long before students fully develop their writing rhythm. You will be teaching control, as well as awareness of legible shapes and clear counters. First introduce the joins that move from the baseline to the tops of *a*, *c*, *d*, *g*, *o*, and *q*. Take care that students move around *a*, *ua*, not through its counter: *ua*.

Examples:

ua ic ug id uq io

Words and suggested sentences to practice: Duane ice ugly hog did Ohio

Duane has an ugly hog.

Did you slide into your Ohio hideout?

9. Next come the diagonal joins that retrace part of a letter at the baseline. Avoid joins that cross through counters: *bu*.

Examples:

bu pi su

Words and suggested sentences to practice: *but pit butter put pat sit sat*

The puppy sits.

Abby put a pat of purple butter on a biscuit.

10. Join both in and out of s, retracing at both the top and bottom of the letter, as shown at the right by the dotted lines. The tops and/or bottoms of s are shortened when a letter joins into it or out of it. That is how the looped cursive s developed. Many students will write an abbreviated s. There is no need to teach this shortening. By not teaching students to shorten the tops and bottoms of s, its basic shape will be retained to a greater degree.

Examples:

is ss

Words and suggested sentences to practice: *is as miss does sassy hiss*

This class never misses.

The sassy snake hisses in Mississippi.

11. Join into e. This join must be taught very precisely, and reviewed whenever it starts to go astray. The exit stroke of a letter preceding e moves up from the baseline, then it twists, changing direction ever so slightly about halfway between baseline and midline, moving around to form the counter of e. See the illustration. Compare the solid line, the curve, to the wiggle in the arm of r. It is this curve that allows e to retain its open counter.

Beware of this configuration. The writing line can go astray and look as if there is something else to read. The slight pause to wonder, "What's that?" slows the reader.

Please see page 50, and Section III, page 17.

Examples:

ie ee

Words and suggested sentences to practice: *me see meet beet pest net*

The green sheep cries in his sleep.

Charles tried to steal the steel eels.

12. Join letters which end at the midline into ascenders. When writing *wh*, keep the last upstroke of *w* in good shape; avoid *who*. One first grade class responded well to a comparison of the upward movement of the ascender with the flight of a seagull. See item 5.

There are no examples of *v* joining to an ascender. *v* rarely precedes a letter with an ascender. There is no keystroke in Barchowsky™ Fluent Hand™ for a *v* with an upstroke line for joining.

A join to *f* requires a retracing movement at the top of *f*.

Examples:

ol wh oh wl ob of

Words and suggested sentences to practice: *old owl who what off often scoff*

I sold the gold owl.

The oboe plays when the owl howls.

Scoff at the often offensive golf offer.

EXCEPTIONS AND PROBLEM JOINS

Joins should be disallowed from letters which end near the baseline into ascenders. The line that would join the letters tends to drag down the height of the ascender, or the length of the connecting line creates too much space. Poor spacing, distorted letters, and the loops that may occur when joining to ascenders reduce legibility. Examples follow for more graphic definition.

- If one joins into *l*, the space becomes too great: *pill*,
  or the ascender of *l* may be pulled down and shortened: *pill*, in which case the two *l* s look like *u*.

- If one joins into *h*, the space will become too great between letters, or the ascender may be so short that *h* looks like *n*: *ah*

- A join from the baseline to *b* might not be so illegible, because a shortened *b* resembles no other letter: *ib*
  However, as said before, it is best to strive for consistent movements.

- A join from the baseline into *f* can create excessive problems, as the writing line travels even farther to retrace the top of *f*: *stiff*

The samples above are written quite carefully. They can be worse:
pill stiff, and *ah* for *ah*.

- No horizontal joins should be made into *e*. This is mentioned in items 1 and 2, regarding crossbars. Neither should one join from o, r, v, or w into *e*.
  Note the distortions that may occur: *oe oe re we*

- Joins should not be made into *z*. Unless *z* is very precisely and slowly written, it will resemble a looped cursive *r*: *z*

- Joins should be discouraged from descenders. There is a tendency for the continuing line of the descender to pull the following letter, to which it is joining, too close: *you*

As personal writing develops, join rules should be enforced only when handwriting becomes illegible, or when it lacks fluency.

HINTS AND COMPARISONS WITH OTHER WRITING SYSTEMS

BFH, A Manual for Fluent Handwriting, is designed for an individual's need to write characters that are easy to form. It provides the means to learn, correct, or improve one's speed and legibility. The more one understands handwriting, the more efficient learning, teaching, and remediating becomes. Handwriting need not follow a model precisely. It just needs clarity and speed. Letters may be round or narrow, tall or short, large or small, and the slant can vary. These differences matter little as long as the characteristics are consistent for each hand. Clear, freely written characters are the goal—never slowly drawn.

Few handwriting programs truly address the needs of small motor development. BFH meets these needs by presenting characters that are easy to form, and need no changes to become cursive. Many programs require beginners to learn print-script, and then to relearn handwriting with a looped cursive style. It is time consuming and damaging to retrain arm, hand, or finger movement for the sole purpose of learning another method, or style of writing which employs characters that must be formed using different directions. Such changes risk confusion. The motor memory of many children interferes with their ability to make directional changes. Slow and/or illegible handwriting results.

If this manual is used to modify, clarify, or speed up a hand already learned, it will be helpful to examine pages 59, 60, and 61. Generic forms of the three most commonly taught alphabet models are compared with Barchowsky™ Fluent Hand™. If one understands the similarities and differences between programs, it will be easier to see just what remediation is needed.

Many alphabet exemplars present lowercase letters that are wider near the baseline than at the tops of letters. Lengthy instruction is often given for entry strokes to each letter, with the emphasis placed on drawing in the area near the baseline. However, it is the tops of letters which are critical. We scan the tops when reading, only referring to the lower portion of a letter when further identification is needed. Try this little experiment. Can you read either of the lines below? They are written by two different methods so you can try to read the one most familiar to you. Then refer to the bottom of the next page. Are either of those lines easier to read?

BFH instruction emphasizes the tops of letters. The movement for letter formation is most efficient if the line of writing shapes the top of the letter, moves down to the baseline, then leaves it as soon as possible, bouncing up to make the next shape, or downstroke. For example, the downstroke of *i* has a small lift at the baseline, the beginning of a bounce for joining *in*. *n* is composed of a downstroke, a bounce up and over and down with a small lift in case it should want to join: *ing*. An easy, rhythmic movement evolves which controls letter shape, as well as spacing.

Most handwriting systems follow tradition rather than logic. We have inherited a notion that one must connect every letter in every word. In actual fact, few adults adhere to this rule because it is easier and faster to lift the pen or pencil now and then. Some programs teach print-script to beginning writers with a transition to looped cursive in second or third grade. Some teach looped cursive from the beginning. Others teach a modified print-script with fewer strokes per letter. These characters can be joined for cursive writing, but the manuals instruct second or third graders to learn a cursive that has the "traditional" look. This cursive requires changes in the ductus of some letters.

Most handwriting systems also adhere to tradition when they recommend exercise patterns. Often such exercises are just not taught. Teachers probably fear that beginning writers will be bored with too much discipline. See the illustration below that demonstrates the irrelevance of some handwriting exercises.

The first is the one most often recommended. Is it designed to train consistent writing, or to train one to write *e* clearly?

Will the exercise deteriorate into something like this sample, as it depends upon scooping along the baseline, and dragging the heel of the hand along in order to join every *e*?

Every BFH exercise pattern relates directly to letter formation. The manual offers many suggestions that make these patterns entertaining, rather than tedious.

BFH capitals and numerals are smaller than those of other hands. Otherwise, most are written at about the same size as those found in other beginning alphabets. Again, most handwriting instruction ignores reason, and goes with tradition when it comes to the capitals

---

Here are the words from the previous page, showing their tops only.

that are taught after a beginning alphabet. If we never encounter the so-called cursive capitals in printed text, why do we cling to capitals that were created for a different time and purpose? Once they were beautiful and fanciful. Their modern counterparts have degenerated into clumsy, often illegible shapes.

The reason that the capitals and numerals are smaller in the sample of Barchowsky™ Fluent Hand™ is to make them more compatible with the size of lowercase letters. They have a better, more readable appearance on a whole page of text. The capitals are de-emphasized and so do not interrupt the eye of the reader. If a teacher finds it easier to teach beginning writers to start the capitals and numerals at the ascender line, it is of little consequence. Probably older students will naturally shorten these characters when they no longer write on paper with lines designated for ascenders and descenders.

There will be, and should be, many deviations from exemplars as children develop their own individual handwriting. Remember, close examination of handwriting can reveal the individual just as a fingerprint can.

Many of us learned a print-script method of writing (sometimes referred to as ball-and-stick or manuscript) before we were introduced to "cursive." Even if there is extensive instruction in a looped cursive method, it is only natural that most of us revert to the print-script we learned first. Some older students and adults manage to write satisfactorily with personal adjustments to print-script. Others have a variety of difficulties.

Print-script, Barchowsky™ Fluent Hand™, and some other models share the same derivation, the humanist hand of the Renaissance. The old, handwritten, humanist letters look very much like the "roman" characters that we read in today's newspapers and books. The handwriting style considered to be "traditional" is looped cursive. It adds loops for joining. It evolved after the Renaissance from copperplate engraving . Flowing lines, loops, and curls were relatively easy to create with engraving tools. Scribes practiced long and hard to imitate the graceful lines, for a hand known as "copperplate." A beautiful looped cursive is not easy to write with today's tools, unless much time and care are devoted to the writing.

The concept of constructing much of an alphabet with circles and straight lines seems simplified and streamlined, especially when the result closely resembles the printed text that we teach children to read. In practice, a round circle and a straight, upright line are not easy to draw—and it is drawing, not writing. Also, the correct placement of the separate parts is a daunting task for a young child. Many children are confused, and put circles on the wrong sides of lines, especially for **b**, **d**, and **p**, creating that nasty problem of reversals. If the letters are written with a continuous line, reversals are extremely rare.

Some educators avoid reversals by teaching a looped cursive alphabet from the very beginning. Reversals are not a problem with either Barchowsky™ Fluent Hand™ or looped cursive because there are no separate parts to assemble. The difference in these two methods is in the movement. Entry strokes, undercurves and overcurves, begin at the baseline, and are emphasized in looped cursive instruction. The strokes have a scooping motion which carries over into the shapes of the letters. It is a slower movement than the direct lift from the baseline for a diagonal join with the BFH method. The critical formation of almost all letters begins at their tops. Therefore the greatest attention should be directed to the midline rather than the baseline. Also, we read from top to bottom and left to right, so if characters are constructed in the same manner, directionality is consistent.

If every letter is joined in every word for looped cursive, there are two problems. First, not all joins work well. For example: **b**, **o**, **v**, and **w** end at the midline, so the writing line must return to the baseline to join some letters. Adjustments must be learned to write some words. *ablong* *oblong*

Second, it is difficult to maintain even, rhythmic movement when joining within long words. Please see Section I, pages 1 and 2, and the second example on page 56. If one writes more than four or five joined letters the heel of the hand tends to drag on the paper, pulling letters off the baseline.

If legibility is a problem with either capitals or numerals, please refer to Sections IV and V. Pages 60 and 61 will help also. Study the ductus of troublesome characters, and practice them as described. Avoid undue repetition; for example, if A is not well formed, practice the pattern ||| ≡ ||| ≡ , and *Arthur Arctic Australia*, etc., rather than A A A , etc. If 5 needs help, practice 5 6 7 5 6 7, etc.

Legible variations of capitals, such as *A B D E F G H J M P R Y* are acceptable, especially for older students. *K*, or any other letter that is hard to read, is not acceptable. Is this sample **K** or **R**?

For those who use a print-script, and need to make their handwriting fluent, or to correct some character formations so that they can join for faster writing with retained, or improved legibility, reference to Section II, Section III, and page 59 will be especially helpful. The addition of exit strokes to letters that will accept them, combined with practice of exercise patterns can make print-script fluent. The most common, and difficult habit to correct is the abrupt stop at the baseline. It is most important to break the habit. Try practicing *uu*, a word such as *mint*, or *ant*; then repeat with the exercise pattern, a word, etc.

A few specific tips and practice words follow.

Note the directions in which the line moves to form circles. If a student follows from **a** to **b**, making the circles in the same way, the bowl of **b** will be written counter-clockwise. No matter, joins from **b** will then be horizontal instead of diagonal, with no loss of legibility unless the bowl opens too far.

Many people write **d** with one stroke so it looks like this: *d*. The writing line starts at the top of the ascender, comes to the baseline, and then forms a counterclockwise bowl. This **d** will still join legibly with letters that follow, so there is no need to change the letter formation.

A join from a counterclockwise **b**, or from any other letter that ends at the midline, into **e** often makes the **e** illegible: *but*

As stated in Section VI, it is valuable to form the habit of using the crossbars of both *f* and *t* to join into letters that follow them. Note in Section III, *f* can be written in a variety of ways, all of which are acceptable because the crossbars will join to letters that follow *f*.

If a young child sees a circle for *o* and fails to hear, understand, or be taught its construction, the letter may start at the baseline. Legibility often suffers with the older student's need to speed up and join letters: *oops*. For some perverse reason, without good instruction at the early stages, one tends to join letters that ought not to join, and not join those that ought to join.

a, *d*, *h*, *k*, *l*, and *z* have exit strokes from which one can join.

am did hip kin like zip

c and *e* are shaped to join easily from the baseline.

cup sheep

Add entry strokes to *j*, *p*, *r*, *v*, *w*, *x*, and *y*.

enjoy up fur ivy sway mix my

Add both entry and exit strokes to *i*, *m*, *n*, and *u*.

him smile any pup

SAMPLES OF COMMON HANDWRITING PROBLEMS

Solutions to these problems will be found in this section, and elsewhere in the manual, especially in Sections I and II. It may be helpful to have this outline too; sometimes just seeing a pertinent sample helps. For self-evaluation older students can check the boxes if they think the problems apply to themselves. Parents and teachers of young children can check off problems that apply to their student(s).

☐ 1. Print-script, all or almost all unjoined. *quick brown*

☐ 2. Writing will not stay on the baseline, the line on which writing should rest. "It is not necessarily expeditious" to stick to one's early admonition to join every letter in every word.

☐ 3. Inconsistent letter slant. Pen or pencil hold may be too tight.

☐ 4. Extenders (the parts of **b, d, f, h, k, l, t** that extend above letters such as **o** and the parts of **f, g, j, p, q, y** and sometimes **z** that extend below the baseline) are too long and/or the space between lines is too small to accommodate them. Try writing on wide lined paper for awhile.

☐ 5. Writing line runs through, rather than around letters.

☐ 6. Excessive forward slant which compresses the counters. Adjust paper position.

☐ 7. Excessively narrow writing, which also compresses counters.

☐ 8. Incorrect construction distorts letters: *poor*. **p** moves incorrectly, and the line for **o** starts at the baseline. *a*

☐ 9. If **a** does not close at the top, it looks like **u**: *u* Also see **g** in 13.
If the second downstroke does not return to the baseline **a** will look like **o**: *a* or *o*.
Is this "boot" or "boat"? *boot*
a with loops through it can be equally confusing. *a a*

☐ 10. If **b**, whether written like this *b*, or this *b*, is too open, it creates legibility problems. *br lr*

☐ 11. **d**, if not closed, looks like **cl**: *cl cl*.

☐ 12. **e** must retain an open counter. It can look like *e* or *l*, but it should not resemble a poorly formed **r**: *r*, an undotted **i**: *i*, or if it gets too tall, an **l**: *l*. Please see Section III, page 17.

☐ 13. If **g** is not closed, it can look like *y*.

☐ 14. **h**, written from the baseline or the top, *h h him*, can be misread if it has no hump. See **m** and **n** in 19.

☐ 15. **h** can be read as **n** if the ascender is too short. *h hi*

☐ 16. **k**, written with two strokes, can look like **K** if the second stroke is too tall: *K*. Stuck in the middle of a word, it appears that you know no better! *LiKe*

☐ 17. *SpRinKLed Capitals* Here capitals are mixed with lowercase letters, a result of using print-script without giving much thought to the results. The sample is legible, but often joins distort letterforms; you can see it happening to the last **a**.

☐ 18. Legibility suffers even more if capitals are used and written very rapidly: *JOIN CAPITALS*

☐ 19. The looped cursive method shows entry strokes on **n** and **m** to be as round as the arches of the letters, which can be confusing: *n m* Arches, not entry strokes should be round. If sharp (*u w*), "arched" **n**'s and **m**'s look like **u**'s and **w**'s. These words are cunning, running, unwilling.

cunning running unwilling

☐ 20. The first **r** is sprung and looks like **v**. The next **r** is shapely, but if it deteriorates, it looks like the last one, an **e**? *v r ι*

☐ 21. *tile* If the crossbar is misplaced, **t** can be hard to read. The word is tile.

☐ 22. If the ends of the upstrokes of **v** and **w** are not pulled in a little (*v w*) they are hard to read, especially when joined: *vim* should read *vim*, and *who* should read *who*.

☐ 23. If the last downstroke of **u** is left off, **u** can look like **v**. *v*

☐ 24. If the space between letters is uneven, the reader is slowed. *spacing*

☐ 25. This spacing is obviously poor also:

Words should not have too much space between them. Cracks occur through which the ⊕ may slip, a problem which can be compounded and expanded.

☐ 26. There should be even, uncrowded margins on both the left and right side of the paper.

There is an all too common inclination to cram words into the right margin which scrunches the writi-
ng.

(margin or edge of paper)

VII 58

COMPARISON OF CHARACTER FORMATIONS

The letterforms on the last pages of this section compare Barchowsky™ Fluent Hand™ with approximations of the three most common writing methods in use in the United States today. You may want to refer to other handwriting manuals for similarities and differences of characters.

This page compares print-script with Barchowsky™ Fluent Hand™. The print-script letters are shown to the left of the BFH letters. Numbers and arrows on the page indicate ductus. If there are no numbers, a letter is written with one stroke. The capitals and numerals in the two methods are similar, so are not shown on this page.

On these two pages, compare the characters of two other popular methods, the grayed characters, with BFH, the black characters. The characters are not exact copies of any one program; they will vary from one manual to the next. The first characters in each set are modified print-script; the lowercase letters have fewer strokes per letter than the letters on page 59. The next characters in each set are looped cursive, and the third are Barchowsky™ Fluent Hand™.

A*a*A	B*b*B	C*c*C	D*d*D
E*e*E	F*f*F	G*g*G	H*h*H
I*i*I	J*j*J	K*k*K	L*l*L
M*m*M	N*n*N	O*o*O	P*p*P
Q*q*Q	R*r*R	S*s*S	T*t*T
U*u*U	V*v*V	W*w*W	X*x*X
Y*y*Y	Z*z*Z		

5 5 5   6 6 6   7 7 7   8 8 8   9 9 9

SECTION VIII

USING Barchowsky™ Fluent Hand™ TYPE

KEYSTROKE INSTRUCTIONS

Although this typeface is presented to assist teachers, children can certainly use it. It is fun for them to write a story or a poem on a computer, and then print the finished product, especially if it resembles handwriting.

Of course, use of the extra keystrokes to make the model look like cursive writing, might be a bit daunting for a very young child, but for an older student, it is both entertaining and instructive.

Barchowsky™ Fluent Hand™ is a font, or typeface. Its use with a manual is strongly recomended. With it, one can type out exemplars for students that complement other subjects in a curriculum. Occasionally, a paper, typed with this font, serves as a useful reminder of good handwriting even if students use the paper for reference only—exemplars do not always need to be traced or copied.

There are alternate strokes in Barchowsky™ Fluent Hand™ that create the joins between letters. For one who is accustomed to typing rapidly, the replication of cursive writing may seem tedious because of the need to use alternate keystrokes. Try typing the text for an exemplar without joins. Then use a spell checker if you wish (software does not recognize alternate keystrokes). Finally, go back and add the keystrokes needed for joining. Page 72 provides a quick, handy reference.

When writing by hand, constant and subtle alterations to most letterforms are made to accommodate spacing, easy joins, and individual abilities and preferences. This font only simulates cursive writing. It is bound by the limitations of type. Subtle movements of the hand give individuality and fluency to handwriting. These movements need no special instruction, but they do need to be understood and observed. If a student's handwriting shows a lack of fluency, the remedy is short sessions of practice using a pattern or letter sequence that relates to whatever has gone awry. The teacher can type out a customized lesson to help that student.

Printouts of exemplars should not be copied endlessly or slavishly. As soon as children learn the basic movements for handwriting, they should only be guided and monitored, so that they maintain clear handwriting that is as rapid as age and physical development allow. Regular, but *never* excessive, practice with patterns should be part of all handwriting instruction.

Barchowsky™ Fluent Hand™ offers only the most essential alternate keystrokes to avoid becoming cumbersome and mind-boggling. However, teachers will sometimes want or need to augment exemplars by editing the printouts by hand. For example, one would expect *o* to join to *t*, but there is no keystroke to fill this need. If you want to show joins for *lot* or *otters*, type the exemplar, then add a small penstroke to show how the line curves up from *o* to *t* : *ot* . Most students will usually join to *t* in this manner even without instruction.

There is no *r* in the Barchowsky™ Fluent Hand™ font that will join to *a*, *o*, *s*, and other letters that require retracing along the tops of the letters in order to join. *r* appears to touch *l*, and other letters with ascenders. There should be no join from *r* to ascenders . The movement would be awkward, and would affect the legibility of *r*. *r* can join to *t*. *t* is short and the dip in the top of *r* moves easily into *t*.

A smart terrier barks at the brown scarf.

Additional information can be found in Section VI, page 44.

At the present time there are no keystrokes to accommodate foreign languages; these will be added in a revision.

Typing instructions for additional or alternate keystrokes will appear as follows:

- **O** indicates option plus the letter.

- **SO** indicates that one holds down both the shift and the option keys while typing the letter.

- Whenever **O** plus two letters is shown, hold down the option key while typing the first letter, release the option key, and press the key for the second letter.

If anything looks odd on a printout, refer back to the instructions in this guide. Most likely, different keystrokes are required. After typing up a few exemplars, you may be surprised by how little time it actually takes. In the process you will have automatically learned quite a lot about how handwriting can work to the best advantage.

KEYSTROKES BETWEEN LETTERS

There are three different keystrokes to form diagonal lines between letters which create the appearance that they are cursive and join.

The lines for simulating joins are shown in the first column. Next are the typing instructions. Explanations of how and where to use lines are in the third column, followed by examples of usage. The same format is used for the exercises (rhythm patterns) and for the alternate characters.

In the lists of letters that precede and follow the joining keystrokes, you will find some of the alternate characters. They are all explained in the next part of this section.

/   O backslash   / for diagonal joins. It can follow all of these letters:

a c d e e e h i i k m m n n u u and *z*
a c d e e e h i i k m m n n u u and *z*

and it can precede:

a c d g i j m n o o o o p q r s u v v w w w x and *y*
a c d g i j m n o o o o p q r s u v v w w w x and *y*

O+ backslash can follow every letter from which you can join diagonally from the baseline except *b, l, p,* and *s*.

in my day nip

/   SO4   Use this for diagonal joins after *b, p,* and *s*, and before all those letters in the second list above, the ones that can receive diagonal joins. Shift+Option+4 will not be used as often as the other two keystrokes for joining. It simulates the retrace around the bowls of *b, p,* and *s*. Some find the need to retrace clumsy. Also there is the danger of running the line through the letters, rather than around, thereby decreasing legibility.

bug sudsy snappy bumpy

In these samples both Option+backslash and Shift+Option+4 were used.

／ SO backslash   Use this keystroke before *t*, and its alternate, *t*. *t* is just a bit taller than letters such as *n* or *u*, yet short enough to allow a natural join from them into *t*. Option+backslash is shaped to meet letters that start near the midline; Shift+Option+backslash is especially shaped to meet *t*. Use it after any letter from which you can join diagonally from the baseline except from *b*, *l*, and *p*. In other words, use Shift+Option+backslash after all of the letters in the second list under Option+backslash.

cut it at enter

Shift+Option+backslash may also be used after *s*. *s* often precedes *t*. The subtle differences between *b*, *p*, and *s* at the baseline, where the line moves around, allow Shift+Option+backslash to fit only *s* well. There is no special keystroke to join *b* or *p* to *t*. If you wish to teach students to join from *b* or *p* to *t*, then it will be necessary to add in the join with a small black mark.

start stop strut doubt abrupt

EXERCISE (RHYTHM) PATTERNS

⁓⁓⁓	**Oui**	⁓⁓⁓ ⁓⁓⁓ ⁓⁓⁓ ⁓⁓⁓ ⁓⁓⁓
uu	**OuU**	uu uu uu uu uu uu
m	**OnN**	m m m m m m
ullullu	**Oio + Oeu**, then repeat **Oeu** for as long as you wish. Add **SO7** (u) at the end.	ullullullullu
mm	**Ono + OnO**, and repeat **OnO** for as long as you wish.	mmmmmmmmmmm
†	**Oia**	† † † † †
∣∣∣ ≡	Repeat capital **I** 3 times, then **Oie**.	∣∣∣ ≡ ∣∣∣ ≡

Other patterns are just composites of characters, their alternates and joining lines.

ccc	c + O backslash + c + O backslash + c	ccc ccc ccc
nunu	n + O backslash + u + O backslash + n + O backslash + u	nunu nunu nunu
sss	s + SO4 + s + SO4 + s	sss sss sss
rrr	r + Or + Or	rrr rrr rrr

ALTERNATE CHARACTERS

Ø   **SOo**   This alternate distinguishes zero (O) from capital O.

Alternate characters are necessary for most letters that join horizontally, such as *o* and *w*. They are also needed for letters which join diagonally from the midline to the ascender line, and because of the varying shapes of some letters.

f   **Of**   The crossbar of this *f* extends out to meet the letter that will follow it. When writing, one automatically adjusts the length of lines which will or will not join horizontally; the handwritten results may be somewhat different from the typed version. See the comments after *o*, the character typed Option zero.

fine friend fur sniff after awful

t   **Ot**   This is the *t* to use for an apparent horizontal join to a letter that will follow.

tire tread tug train twin letter pitfall

i   **Oii**   Entry strokes must be eliminated following horizontal joins. This *i*, and many of the following alternate letters have no entry strokes. Only samples are given, as the explanation for each is the same as for Oii.

fine tire fit tin oil devil

j   **Oj**   *project Mojave fjord*

m   **Om**   *Tom Mom some*

n   **Onn**   *on turn bony onion burn catnip*

p   **SOp**   *top stop opera opinion*

r	**Or**	*freight train track trail or for*
u	**So7**	*funny turn ouch*
ʋ	**Ov**	*cover serve oven love*
ʋ̄	**SOv**	This ʋ has a serif. It also has a line extending to the right to make a horizontal join from it. *ivy vote vine*
ʋ̄	**Oue**	Use this one if there is a horizontal join both before and after ʋ. *bovine survive*
w	**Ow**	*cow know snow*
w̄	**SOw**	This w has a serif, and is used like SOv (ʋ̄). *won wow*
w̄	**SO2**	This w is used like Oue (ʋ̄). *own known frown*
w′	**Oq**	Here is a diagonal join moving from the midline to the ascender line. Use this w′ when wondering… *who what where why* and for *whole whales*
w′	**SOq**	Use this w′ after a horizontal join and before a join to the ascender line. *fowl owl*
x	**SO9**	*ox oxen fox*
y	**Oy**	*joy cry mighty*

σ	**O zero**	This σ will simulate the many horizontal joins needed from it. Typed horizontal joins appear to be straight lines moving from one letter to the next: *on one*. The students' horizontal lines can bend a bit more, and probably will. The only dangers are excessive loops and swoops: *coat* . Note that, in the sample, lines cross through letters and damage legibility. The length of horizontal joins may also vary with individual fluency and letter spacing. Remember, the name of the game is always to move from letter to letter as easily and legibly as possible.

ooze groan Rover growl

σ́	**O9**	As with *w* and *w*, this o will join to ascenders.

gold oboe

σ́	**SOk**	Because of the shape of the top of *f*, and because we write *of* so often, this σ́ is used; it moves more smoothly into *f* than O9 (σ́). The two samples at the left appear to be identical, but if one tries O9 with *f* the difference is clear, especially when enlarged: *of*

of off often soft

ℯ	**Oee**	e is the only letter that begins halfway between the midline and the baseline. Because of this difference in formation and shape, it needs two alternates to allow letters to join into *e* from the baseline. Use this one for diagonal joins after:

a c d e ℯ h i i k l m m n n u u and z.

Caesar me he the need field

ℯ	**SO3**	As explained for SO4 (∕), the shapes at the baseline of *b*, *p*, and *s* require a slightly different diagonal join. e follows these letters so often that it is best to have an alternate character so that one can easily choose to teach, or not to teach, the join from *b*, *p*, and s to *e*.

be bet pen open seal season

l   **Ol**   The end of *l* is rounded, and just different enough in shape to need a special character for the appearance of a smooth join. Note that *l* and *t* have similar endings, but *t* joins with its crossbar.

line slime lute lot

l   **Ouo**   The difference in the shapes of the two *l*s at the left is nearly imperceptible until put to use. Ouo is used to simulate a join to an ascender. In most flowing handwriting the line at the end of *l* drifts up, and appears to join. Actually it only meets the downstroke of an ascender, and touches the ascender that follows it. This *l* also works well when *l* preceeds *t*. As *t* is so short, *l* will often join, but the stretch is greater than it is to letters that end at the midline.

all Alfred tilting malt

A summary follows on page 72.

KEYSTROKE SUMMARY

∅	**SOo** alternate numeral O		υ	**Ov** follows horizontal join
/	**O backslash** most diagonal joins		ʊ	**SOv** to join into letters
/	**SO backslash** to join to t		ʊ	**Oue** follows horizontal join & joins into letters
/	**SO4** join from b, p, s		w	**Ow** follows horizontal join
e	**Oee** to join into e		w	**SOw** to join into letters
e	**SO3** to join into e from b, p, s		w	**SO2** follows horizontal joins & joins into letters
f	**Of** to join into letters		w	**Oq** to join into ascenders
i	**Oii** follows horizontal join		w	**SOq** follows horizontal join & to join into ascenders
j	**Oj** follows horizontal join		x	**SO9** follows horizontal join
l	**Ol** to join into letters		y	**Oy** follows horizontal join
l	**Ouo** to simulate join into ascenders and t			
m	**Om** follows horizontal join			
n	**Onn** follows horizontal join		**EXERCISE PATTERNS:**	
σ	**Ozero** to join into letters		uni	**Oui**
ở	**O9** to join into ascenders		uu	**OuU**
ở	**SOk** to join into f		m	**OnN**
p	**SOp** follows horizontal join		ullullu	**Oio + Oeu + SO7**
r	**Or** follows horizontal join		mm	**Ono + OnO**
u	**SO7** follows horizontal join		†	**Oia** for capitals
t	**Ot** to join into letters		‖‖‖ ≡	Capital **I** 3 times + **Oie** for capitals

PRACTICE WORDS AND SENTENCES

If you want ideas for extra practice, refer to this section for suggestions of letters and sequences of letters. Create any others that are relevant to current studies, interests or fads. Practice is most productive when it is relevant.

Words are shown in Barchowsky™ Fluent Hand™. If a student is working to improve, but not change, a previously learned writing method, it may be best to present words and sentences verbally, or in a type one might see in a book, or in a corrected version of his or her accustomed hand. Letters are shown joined as prescribed in Section VI. Please refer to that section, especially if you are teaching beginning students, and want unjoined versions of letters.

A a

An ape ate a grape.   Aggravated alligators attack aqua aliens.
Agatha gave an apple to Arty, the aardvark.   Alan ambled to Alabama.

B b

Bill's bus bent Betty's bumper.   Blue, bulbous buffoons battle in Britain.
Black bears build bungalows in Bolivia.   Barbara blows blue bubbles.

C c

Coco is cute.   Cows chew clover.   Claude carries clocks to Calcutta.
Catch a cautious crow covering his coat with coconut cream.

D d

Dwight dives in Denver.   Diana's delicious date dumplings are dessert.
Don't dawdle by the dairy door.   Dangerous Dan drives a Dodge.

E e

Eels have green knees.   Sheep bleat.   Ellen rides elevators in Egypt.
Enter the East Empire eagerly.   Evan sees an eclipse of Earth.

F f

Fred fusses.   Fanny, the fox, fluffs her fine soft fur.
Fly to France.   Feed friendly Frank the frozen fish fillet.

G g

Greet Greta if she giggles.   Gus grabbed great gooey gumdrops.
George grows grapes in Georgia.   A gaggle of gray geese gropes for grubs.

H h

Hurry to help Harriet.   Herman hikes and hides high in the Himalayas.
Horace hugs his horrid hog.   Hush! Hilda will hear her howling hyena.

I i

Ice cream is nice.   Each inch of Izzy, Ida's inchworm, is itchy.
Ike likes icicles.   Ira imagined living in windy Ireland in winter.

J j

Joyce jumped a jolly jet.   Janet enjoys juggling jugs in the jungle.
Jelly and juice are in the jam.   Just jump on a jaguar to go to Jamaica.

K k

Kate likes to fly kites.   Karen picked kicking chickens.
Ken's backstroke cracked the 14 karat kakapo.   Kangaroos kick King Kong.

L l

Lila loves lollipops.   Lola likes llamas who play a London lullaby.
Lisa loads llamas into lorries.   Sally slides into millions of malls.

M m

My mop is muddy.   Mousey ate a monster in Muncie.
Manuel munches gummy jam in Mom's major movie.

N n

Ned eats no bananas in Nevada.   Nine, not ten pennies are never new.
Nora reads a new novel.   Nanook of the North ran north to Nepal.

P p

Peel pink paper puppets.   Pappy paints pink poppies purple for Paul.
A pink pig puts on purple pants.   Pepita paused in Paris.

Q q

Queen Quentin is quiet.   We have a quota of aqua quail.
Question the queen.   Quasimodo was in a quandary in Quebec.

R r

Harry, Larry, and Rory hurry.   Red raccoons ran a race to Rome.
Row a red raft on the river.   Roll round, red barrels on a rough road.

S s

Sassy Susie is silly.   Sasha sat on soggy stumps to see the sunrise.
Stuff sixty sausages.   Sue slipped in Mississippi, not in Saskatchewan.

T t

The turtle tells tall tales. Tom put twenty tiny tops in a tree in Turkey.
Two tin, tinted, tooting trucks are on the train. Try the putty in Teheran.

U u

Ursula is an umpire. Unicorns are usually in the underbrush.
Use an umbrella in Utah. Undo the ugly, grumpy mule.

V v

Vera swings on a vine. Vinnie drives a very heavy van over the Volga.
Van saved the vapor in a vacuum vat. Violet visited Venice.

W w

Where are the willows? What is Willy doing in the whirling snow?
Why is it windy in Warsaw? Who won the worst war in the West?

X x

Dixie exits. Xerxes fixes mixed boxes.
Examine the six fixtures in Mexico. Xavier fixed the xylophone.

Y y

Yell loudly to Mary. Yasmin says the lazy yak yawns in the yard.
Yvonne stays in Yemen for many days. Yellow yams are yonder.

Z z

Zachary is zany. Zebras get dizzy in Zambia and Zaire.
Zealots count to zero in Venezuela. Zed zig-zags.

WORDS WITH COUNTERCLOCKWISE LETTERS, THE *u* FAMILY

ugly	you	add	dog	glue	quote
dug	yell	age	dude	goo	quay
cut	yet	ate	duty	gooey	quad
due	yellow	alley	dye	gull	aqua
tug	day	adage	duel	gaudy	quota
lug	yew	adequate	ducat	gag	quell
cocoa	old	eat	lot	too	valley
cool	out	edge	let	tell	vale
cage	oval	equate	log	told	vat
coat	ogle	elevate	lug	tug	vacate
clay	ogee	ecology	lull	tag	vault
cloud	octave	equal	leg	toot	velvet
wow	wave	weave	wove	wall	waggle

WORDS WITH CLOCKWISE LETTERS, THE *n* FAMILY

Vowels are added in this group.

nip	imp	rip	him	kin	bump
nap	mink	rib	hip	kink	bum
numb	mop	rub	hum	krypton	bike
nib	mine	ribbon	hump	kipper	banner
number	mime	rhubarb	hemp	kimono	bummer
nine	umpire	run	hammer	kabuki	bunk
pump	prop	pun	punk	pop	prim

WORDS WITH CROSSBAR JOINS

tie	fine	kitty	goofy	twig	thoughtful
city	fin	mighty	stuffy	truck	catfish
tire	fish	beauty	puffy	treat	nutmeg
tight	five	misty	gruff	free	Batman
tile	nifty	glitter	cuff	fuss	wolfman
tug	tiny	gift	gritty	waffle	catnip

HORIZONTAL JOINS

HORIZONTAL JOINS FROM r

on	some	opal	rim	rise	yarn
or	bone	write	ring	right	mirror
over	core	wrong	rug	barn	flurry
come	visit	own	rivet	farm	ruse
one	vine	cone	rub	ripe	charm
onion	wit	opinion	try	strawberry	cry

DIAGONAL JOINS THAT REQUIRE RETRACING

ace	pig	busses	big	bison	success
mice	puppy	brassy	bug	past	bumpy
great	pond	messy	misspelled	possessions	bath

JOINS WITH e

SOME LETTERS SHOULD NOT JOIN WITH e

me	sent	keep	never	toe	feet
he	leopard	sleep	even	doe	ten
she	heap	deep	wet	hoe	seven
jest	dear	greet	west	river	rent
meat	deer	speed	feast	rest	ever
meet	sheep	jeep	fed	test	tempt

JOINS FROM THE MIDLINE TO ASCENDERS

old	who	stroke	mold	where	poke
gold	what	stoke	told	when	oboe
fold	why	whole	okra	of	offer

mm, nn, mn & nm

sunny	mummy	grammar	inmate	manner	column
bunny	gummy	comma	unmade	uncanny	solemn
banner	inning	hammer	immense	unmanned	condemn

WORDS TO HELP DISTINGUISH cl FROM d.
If not well defined, dog can look like clog.

day clay	dot clot	dub club	down clown	duster cluster
dash clash	dear clear	dip clip	dock clock	dump clump
dank clank	dove clove	damp clamp	dunk clunk	dapper clapper

WORDS WITH JOINS FROM v AND w
The movement on the upstroke often needs practice to keep v and w legible.

victory	vast	flavor	wig	wrap	warn
video	vowel	evident	wild	wreck	wage
viola	vote	vault	wigwam	wise	wallop

WORDS WITH JOINS FROM c TO o CORRECT THE FORMATION OF o

cow	coach	cowpoke	cook	concoct	cozy
cost	common	cowboy	coconut	contract	coupon
cord	cold	coyote	cookie	compose	concourse

WORDS TO HELP DISTINGUISH j FROM J AND k FROM K AND p FROM P

Jill	jinx	June	Kay	slick	Ken
Japan	jar	juice	Karl	sink	keyboard
Jamaica	jam	July	Klondike	kin	Kiev
John	jolly	jug	Kansas	kazoo	trick
Judy	enjoy	Jenny	Kasper	chicken	Kennedy
Jupiter	inject	jelly	Kentucky	blink	clickety-clack

Pablo	Peru	happy	papoose	panda	Peoria
Patty	Phillip	paper	people	Plato	stopper
Pago Pago	Persia	papaya	topper	philosopher	Pepita

COMPOUND WORDS

Compound words often need more practice. As one automatically thinks of two separate words making one word, there is a tendency to leave too much space between the two parts, especially if there is no easy join between the parts. *bathtub* is easier than *breakfast*.

yourself	elsewhere	sunshine	become	piecrust	baseball
broadcast	spotlight	blindfold	instead	wishbone	football
myself	railroad	sunset	beside	snowman	faultless
classmate	nonstop	midnight	cannot	jigsaw	necktie
bookcase	fishhook	bathroom	cowpoke	goldfish	rowboat
suitcase	footprint	toothbrush	handmade	fishbone	however

GLOSSARY

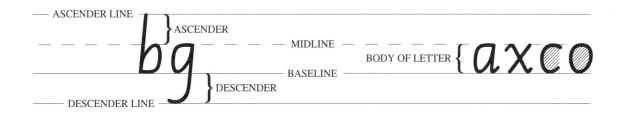

ascender	the part of tall letters which extends above the midline. *b*, *d*, *f*, *h*, *k*, and *l* have ascenders. *t* extends just a bit above the midline; it is not considered to have an ascender.
ascender line	guideline on paper for beginning writers which defines the height of ascenders.
baseline	guideline on any lined paper on which the bodies of letters sit.
body	portion of a letter that occupies the space between midline and baseline; also known as the **x** height, or the space occupied by a lowercase *x*.
counter	space enclosed by the line that defines the body of a letter; white space defined by any line or lines. See the shaded portions of *c* or *o* in the example above.
cursive	as defined by <u>Random House Dictionary</u>, 1987: "handwriting in flowing strokes with the letters joined together." In this manual, cursive is interpreted as flowing, but without a demand that every letter in every word be joined. See <u>looped cursive</u>.
descender	the part of letters which extends below the baseline. *f*, *g*, *j*, *p*, and *y* have descenders.
descender line	guideline on paper for beginning writers which defines the length of descenders.
ductus	sequence and direction of strokes by which letters are written.
exemplar	a sample or model to which a student refers or copies.

extender	an extension of the writing line, either above the midline, or below the baseline, an ascender or descender.
font	a particular point size and style of a typeface, such as bold, condensed, or italic. In computer language, the term font usually refers to a typeface, disregarding the size and style.
italic	hand developed in the Renaissance, or of the Italian. The exemplar alphabets in this manual are based on italic models. It also refers to type which is slanted, usually for emphasis.
join	As used in this manual, "join" refers to the movement from letter to letter without lifting the pen or pencil from the paper. "Join" commonly refers to a connection of two parts. Think of movement that flows from letter to letter, rather than the attachment of two separate parts.
ligature	connection between letters. See "join."
looped cursive	handwriting methods that are commonly referred to as "cursive." Looped ascenders and descenders and a forward slant are characteristic of these hands. Usually all letters in each word are joined.
lowercase	small letters. The term originates from the storage of lead type characters. The small letters were stored in a case below the capital, or uppercase letters. To avoid confusion when referring to handwriting that may be large or small, the term lowercase is used throughout this manual.
midline	top of bodies of letters, usually defined on paper for beginning writers by a dotted or dashed line; also "waistline."
point size	a designation for the size of letters in type.
typeface	an alphabet designed for printing.
serif	an entry or exit stroke, or any small mark, extension, or enlargement at the beginning or end of a typed or handwritten letter stroke.